"Most of the experience of those who have been afflicted with leprosy in Hawai'i—the anguish and bereavement, and also the hope and loves and courage—has never been told. A truly personal account from within that history is a rare and precious human document. We are all indebted to Henry Nalaielua for the intimacy and candor of this narrative, and to Sally-Jo Bowman, who helped to bring it into words."

— **W.S. Merwin**, Pulitzer Prize For Poetry (*The Carrier of Ladders*)

"Henry Nalaielua is surely a *kupuna* of the centuries, whose aloha is unconditional, even through times of escalating changes for Native Hawaiians. A historian, storyteller, composer, musician, singer, artist, diplomat and politically savvy health care advocate— this is how I know Uncle Henry. *No Footprints in the Sand* will now be woven into our history—for all who call Hawai'i home. A must read for Hawai'i health care providers."

— **Emmett Aluli**, Moloka'i physician

"*No Footprints in the Sand* is the inspiring story of a life well lived despite physical affliction, separation from family, the injustice of exile. Henry Nalaielua has faced the challenges of that life with courage, honesty, dignity, and unfailing good humor. In the whole history of Kalaupapa there have been but a handful of books by, or about, the ordinary people who lived and died on that painful shore. *No Footprints in the Sand* ranks among the best."

— **Alan Brennert**, *Moloka'i*

NO FOOTPRINTS
IN THE SAND

A Memoir of Kalaupapa

NO FOOTPRINTS IN THE SAND
A MEMOIR OF KALAUPAPA

BY HENRY KALALAHILIMOKU NALAIELUA
WITH SALLY-JO KEALA-O-ĀNUENUE BOWMAN

WATERMARK
PUBLISHING

ISBN-10: 0-9779143-0-5
ISBN-13: 978-0-9779143-0-2

Library of Congress Control Number:
2006932700

DESIGN
Jayson Harper
Darin Isobe
Lora Lamm
PacificBasin Communications

PRODUCTION
Maggie Fujino

EDITOR
Tamara Leiokanoe Moan

COVER PHOTOGRAPHY
Monte Costa
Hawaiʻi State Department of Health (inset)

BACK COVER PHOTOGRAPHY
Ray Jerome Baker/Bishop Museum

All paintings by Henry Nalaielua,
    reproductions courtesy of
    Kaʻohulani McGuire and Lianne Sing

Additional photos courtesy of
    Anwei Law Skinsnes, IDEA

Watermark Publishing
1088 Bishop Street, Suite 310
Honolulu, HI 96813

TELEPHONE Toll-free 1-866-900-BOOK
WEB SITE www.bookshawaii.net
EMAIL sales@bookshawaii.net

Printed in the United States

Contents

For Gena

Prologue

Kalaupapa 2006

This wind-beaten peninsula off the rugged north coast of Moloka'i juts into wild seas, bounded at its back by cliffs nearly 2,000 feet high. The elements dominate—ocean, sky, wind, rain, the cycles of the sun by day and year, the stars and moon by night. In the absence of much "civilization," it's easy to feel the natural power of the earth. Today's visitors often remark on the peace and serenity of the place, rare qualities in the twenty-first century.

But this small triangle of land is known more for its historical sorrow as Hawai'i's leper settlement, though it also has another history long predating that. Since 1984 it has been both a Hawai'i State Health Department facility and a U.S. National Historical Park, with park access limited to guided tours.

Henry Kalalahilimoku Nalaielua, Jr. has lived in this place most of the last seven decades. He spent only his first ten years with his family. His parents—Henry Sr., half-Hawaiian and half-Chinese, and Annie Helelā Nalaielua, three-fourths Hawaiian and maybe part Tahitian—had Henry and five older children. When Henry was diagnosed with Hansen's disease in 1936, the news was a virtual death sentence to a prison from which there would be neither escape nor parole. The crime: Leprosy. The ultimate prison: Kalaupapa.

In 1866 the first "shipment" of patients arrived at Kalaupapa under the new Hawaiian Kingdom quarantine law that tried to address the burgeoning epidemic that affected mostly native Hawaiians. Until the mid-twentieth century, health authorities insisted the disease was virulently contagious. Every experimental treatment came to naught. For those reasons, almost no patients ever returned from the Settlement.

For many decades, the disease was called by its Biblical name, leprosy. Now it's called Hansen's disease. Since the late 1940s modern antibiotic drugs have controlled or cured it. And medical researchers have discovered it's not nearly so contagious as people used to think.

In the century of sorrow, more than 8,000 patients came to the Settlement. The last new patients arrived in 1969.

The Settlement's population peaked in 1890 at 1,213, a figure that included *kokua*, or healthy individuals who came voluntarily with family members diagnosed with the disease. Some 8,000 are buried in the seaside graveyard or near the churches. Now Kalaupapa's population is less than 100. Fewer than 30 are patients, the rest medical professionals or other service personnel. With more historic buildings than people, Kalaupapa is a ghost town in the making.

When Henry came here as a kid of 15—after 5 years in Kalihi Hospital, a Hansen's disease quarantine station on Oʻahu—it was bigger than most shoreline villages in Hawaiʻi, and not unlike them in many ways. But he couldn't help but notice one big difference.

The sand beach that stretches nearly a mile beyond the wharf was always laid smooth by the tide. Hansen's disease plays havoc with feet, ulcerating them, crippling them. Such feet walk poorly. And in sand they cannot walk at all. Most patients in Henry's time left no footprints in that golden sand. In a few more years, he would be among those unable to walk the beaches.

Now Henry is 80, born November 3, 1925. The oldest patients are 99, the two youngest, 63. Soon the Settlement will be nothing but history.

I first met Henry in 1993, when we both happened to be staying overnight as guests of Dr. Emmett Aluli at his Hawaiian Homestead home near Hoʻolehua on topside Molokaʻi. I was working on a magazine project with Emmett. Henry had attended meetings of a health board on which he sat with the doctor, and would fly down to Kalaupapa the next morning.

Fortunately I took Henry's address and phone number, because two years later I needed him. In 1995 I got two magazine assignments to write about Kalaupapa. The person I thought would be the key to spending extended time there was not available. Henry was my long shot. Would he remember me? Would he be receptive?

I called, establishing who I was in my family in that classic Hawaiian way reminiscent of our forebears reciting their genealogies at first meeting. I knew that, because of many regulations, most visitors to Kalaupapa spend only four hours there. I told Henry that to do a proper job of my assignments I would need two or three days at Kalaupapa. And I would need to bring photographer Monte Costa with me.

A silence followed on the phone. I was thinking, "If he doesn't help me, I'll have to tell those editors I promised them stories I can't produce."

Then Henry spoke. "Sure, I'll help you. I'll sponsor you to stay at the Visitors' Quarters. When do you want to come?"

In May of 1995 Monte and I spent two nights at the vintage-1930 Visitors' Quarters. For most of our time Henry took us here and there in his Chevy truck, driving us over roads that are scarcely more than tracks while the notes I took bounced and scrawled over more than 100 pages. The four-hour tour he used to give paying customers stretched into three days as we crawled down into the Old Woman's Cave at the edge of the deep blue sea and up onto the remains of an ancient *heiau* (temple), places that most visitors never get near. Inside Siloama Church Henry pointed out the bellpull. He grabbed the end of it, tied in a loop rather than a knot.

"This is for hands like these," he said, thrusting his fist into the loop. I had not noticed before that his hands have "crabbed," fingers curling permanently into the palms, a classic problem with Hansen's disease. Crabbing happened slowly to Henry's fingers, a fact he simply ignores. He picks up a pencil or brush with his left hand, fixes it between the fingers and thumb of his right hand, and goes right on drawing, painting, or writing in elegant script.

One evening, as we were cleaning up our supper dishes in the visitors' kitchen, he came back by, bearing three volumes of the Kalaupapa Historical Society's picture albums. The three of us all pored over every page.

In our days with Henry, Monte and I learned much about Kalaupapa's past and present, and even a glimmer of the future. And just by being with him, we learned about Henry himself and came to love him. After that, Monte and I both stayed in touch with him.

Henry gave us freely and completely all that we needed and more. So it was without hesitation that I said "Yes" when he and his friend Gena Sasada approached me in 2000 about helping him write this book.

In the course of working on it, I came to know Henry much more deeply. He is by nature stubbornly willful. That trait at times betrayed him into defiant but stupid decisions. But it also kept him from bitterness and self-pity. I began to perceive and appreciate Henry's strong and independent intellect, and his talent as a natural artist and musician. I saw that those main fibers—art, music, articulate intelligence, along with love and loss, sickness and health—ran through his life as themes, rounding turning points both obvious and subtle as the years went by.

It is my honor and privilege to have shaped this story, to have coaxed more out of Henry's prodigious memory than he put in his first drafts, to have helped recreate scenes and conversations, to have put the narrative in order and historical context.

In that respect I am the co-author. But the story is Henry's, his legacy, from the place of exile where he found no footprints in the sand.

– Sally-Jo Keala-o-Ānuenue Bowman, 2006

The Time Before

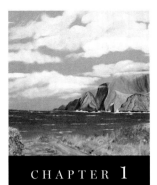

CHAPTER 1

Nīnole 1930

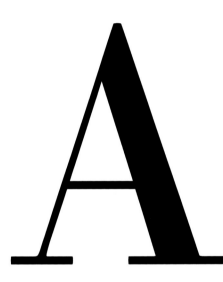

little village sits among acres and acres of sugar cane fields on the Big Island's Hāmākua Coast. It is marked by gulches, bridges, plantation camps, villages and narrow-gauge railroad tracks. I watched my father and brothers get up every morning up at 4:00 a.m. They left the house by 6:00 to work on Honohina Sugar Plantation. Dad was a luna—a field supervisor.

I was the youngest of us all. Too little to go with them, so I stayed with Mama and Evelyn and Christina, my sisters. They would be in the kitchen washing dishes from the men's breakfast and preparing the next breakfast, for themselves and me.

One day in November 1927, when I was only two years old, we took a boat trip to Honolulu and went to a place where we left my sister, Evelyn. She was the oldest of us all, 16. In three days we went back home. I felt sad that she wasn't with us, but Mama told me it was normal for someone to go away. After awhile I didn't miss her anymore.

Christina was only a year and a half older than me, the next-to-youngest of us. After Evelyn left, the two of us went with Mama everywhere. We'd go down to the rivers to catch freshwater shrimp, fish and shellfish – ʻopae, oʻopu and hihiwai. We even picked hoʻiʻo, ferns we ate raw with our freshwater catch. Christina and I had a pet pig, Puaʻa, that would sleep in a box in our bedroom. When he got big enough, he was killed for a lūʻau. Only we didn't know that until several days after the lūʻau. We cried when we found out, but there was nothing we could do. I think if we had known before the lūʻau, we would not have been able to eat.

After that, we had a small brown and white poi dog named Kalakoa for his calico coloring. He slept with us under the covers in the four-poster bed with the mosquito net. We loved him.

But at feeding time, we'd say:

"Your turn!"

"Not! Your turn!"

"Ho, supposed to take chance every day. I went feed him yesterday."

We went with Uncle John when he blasted fish near the mouth of the streams we called Akahawai. He'd set up electrical wires in the water and give the fish a big jolt to numb them. Then he could wade in and pick up the āholehole. Sometimes he used a throw net for mullet.

Uncle John, who was Mama's youngest brother, lived with us. He wasn't much of a talker and he seldom sat down with the family in the house. Mostly, he drank beer. And he loved to fish. He was my favorite uncle. At the ocean, we'd go on the rocks. He'd tell Christina and me to wait right there. In about an hour, he'd be back with a bag of ʻopihi—the limpets Hawaiians love to eat raw—and we'd go home. Wherever we went—Honohina, Hakalau, Honomū, Akaka Falls, Wailea—those were my best days as a kid.

Sometimes we saw my Tūtū Helelā, Mama's mother, and she spoke Hawaiian to me. At home my mother and father spoke Hawaiian to each other, but never to us. That was in the days when a lot of Hawaiians thought it was foolish or even dangerous to speak our own language. Adults at the time—my parents included—remembered 1893, when haole businessmen in the Hawaiian Kingdom overthrew the monarchy. A few years later the U.S. annexed the Kingdom as a territory. The message was that old ways were no good, reinforced when the new powers forebade the Hawaiian language in schools. I didn't know any of that, and I was too busy being a little rascal to think much about who spoke Hawaiian and when. I was the only one of all us kids who spoke Hawaiian, and only with my Tūtū.

Once I decided to drink a bottle of the home brew my father kept in the dining room cabinet. He had too many bottles to miss one. He'd probably think he'd drunk it himself. Christina was there, and she said she'd tell Dad.

She watched me pour the beer into a tall glass. I drank a little. I already felt sick. Really SICK. I thought of dumping the rest down the kitchen sink, but I decided Mama would smell it. So I flushed it down the toilet. Then I threw the bottle out the door into the cane field, and washed the glass so hard I almost broke it. I put the glass back in the cupboard.

Christina never did tell Dad. My home brew adventure was our secret.

Then one day early in 1933 Christina sailed away with our secret. She was nine. Mama, Aunt Rachel and my two middle brothers, David and Robert, went with her. This time, I stayed at home with my Dad. My oldest brother, Joseph, and I asked questions.

"Where is Christina going? Why is she gone?"

"You're too young," my father said to me. "You don't need to know."

"I miss her," I said. "How come I can't go?"

"You're too young to go where your sister's going."

It was confusing. I was seven. I wanted answers and I didn't get any. I had a dreadful feeling Christina wasn't coming back, just like Evelyn. Who would go with me to the river?

I was still sad by the time Mama came home several days later without Christina and Robert. She told me, "Don't worry. Christina will be fine."

"Where is she now?" I asked.

"On another island with all her new friends."

This whole thing was getting stranger to me. "Why can't I go?" I asked.

"They don't allow boys over there," Mama said.

"Robert isn't here at home. Where is he if he isn't here?"

She didn't tell me Robert was in Honolulu. She just said, "You're too young to understand. Now no more questions."

So now, instead of five of us kids being home, just three of us were left, Joseph, the oldest boy, and David, who was a couple years older than Christina, and myself.

I was naturally naughty, like most little boys. I sneaked open the screened food safe door or the lid on the big crock and snacked on whatever was inside. My favorite was salted *'opae*, the little freshwater shrimp. And *pipi kaula*, beef jerky. And poi.

Anything off-limits appealed to me too. I'd take a shovel or a pickax from the tool shed and maybe dig a hole in the cane field. I never put the shovel back. Just left it in the cane field. My father thought he'd forgotten it somewhere.

I monkeyed with the typewriter he used to write letters, putting in paper and typing nonsense. It was fun watching the carriage move—until I jammed it up. Then I ripped out the paper and threw it away.

Some days I'd take my Lionel electric train out in the cane field with part of the track and the engine, flat car, sleeper and caboose. Without electricity, I'd push the cars along the track I laid out in the red dirt.

I'd fool with the musical instruments my father had around the house, mostly stringed instruments. He had been a bandmaster in the Army during World War I and when he mustered out, he brought a lot of instruments with him. We had a piano, bass, guitar and 'ukulele and he brought sax, trumpet, French horn, flute and piccolo, I remember. I learned to play some by ear and I sang with my brothers. They had a trio, and once I went with them to sing at a party.

We were Catholic, but we only went to Mass maybe once in three months, even though we lived within sight of the church. I did make my First Communion.

At last I was old enough to go to school. I couldn't wait to get out of the house. But when I got to first grade at John M. Ross School, it was hell. At least the first week was. When the teacher told me to go up to the blackboard, I was scared to grab the chalk because I didn't know what it was or what I was supposed to do with it. Even worse, I couldn't add or subtract to save my hide. In fact, from my seat, I couldn't see the blackboard. I'd get up to the board and find out the teacher had put up "4 + 6." Nobody discovered until more than a year later that I was terribly nearsighted.

But gradually I caught on, and began to enjoy school more.

Mama made us wear shoes to school, but halfway to school I'd throw them in the bushes. After school I'd pick them up.

I found other exciting things to do. By the time I was ten, I started smoking my brothers' Lucky Strikes, Camels and Chesterfields. I'd steal a pack or two, and one brother would always blame another. Even my mother didn't think I was the thief.

I became a pro at smoking, just by watching my brothers. At John M. Ross School in Ninole my friends and I would smoke in the boys' bathroom or under the school building. We never got caught. At home I'd smoke in the house when my father was at work and Mama was out too, careful that my brothers didn't catch me either.

I even took Uncle John's Bull Durham! But not too much, because I had to roll my own.

Once one of my dad's field workers was heading to a section of cane to be cut. On my way home from school one day, I saw him leading a mule. He said, "Eh! You like ride?"

I nodded.

"Jump on top."

He boosted me up and he led the mule to my house.

In Honohina, the "tin can" theater roofed in corrugated metal showed movies for the plantation workers. Lots of them were silent films. The first one I saw was *King Kong*. I remember one of the Filipinos who worked for my father called it "Kong Kong."

Sometimes the doorman would know who I was—he knew my Dad or one of my brothers—and he'd say, "Oh, I know you. Come." So I got in free.

The kid price was 15 cents, but I counted on getting in free. Sometimes the theater showed cowboy movies.

In the spring of fourth grade I got sick and wasn't able to go to school. I remember taking a steam bath every other day while I was at home. Mama boiled water on the stove, then made a tent of a blanket for me to sit under with a tin bucket of boiling water with eucalyptus leaves in it. I'd sit there, breathing the choking steam for a half hour at a time.

But the steam didn't help. Every place Mama touched on my body was sore. She took me to Hilo to see this Hawaiian doctor, Dr. Kaonohi. He made me take some strange greenish medicine that tasted funny, but it didn't help either.

After some weeks my Mom and I took the boat to Honolulu. We stayed with my cousin Rachel. Her mother, Aunt Rachel, was Mama's sister. While we were there, she gave me more liquid medicine and took me to Dr. Chung-Hoon. The part I liked best was riding on the trolley. We didn't have trolleys anywhere on the Big Island.

If she knew what sickness I had, she wasn't saying. Everything was hush-hush.

We stayed until after Easter vacation. I didn't feel a whole lot better and knew something was wrong with me. My feet were so painful I couldn't walk barefoot. Sores opened on the backs of my calves and they were hard to heal. Mama tried all kinds of medicines and nothing worked. I had the pain, the sores, the medicine—and the "blahs." I went back to school in May.

Not long after, the district school nurse came, going from class to class checking on all the kids. I think it was a Monday. I was sitting in the front row of my class. She stood before me and studied my face.

Then she said, "Henry, do you see that chair in the corner of the room?"

"Yes."

"I want you to sit there until I come back for you."

I went to the chair and sat down. Then she talked to my teacher, and when she was through she told my whole class, "You can all go home now for today. Except you, Henry. I want you to stay."

I thought she was selecting me for something special. I wondered where the rest of the class had gone.

The nurse walked over to me. My teacher was still in the room.

"Is your mother at home?"

"Yes."

"Is your father still at work?"

"Yes," I said.

"Does your family have a telephone?"

"Yes." This was getting tiresome. "Do you know the number?"

"Yes," I said. "Sixteen-W-three. Two longs and one short."

She told me to stay there, and she left the room. When she came back, she said she would take me home.

She had called Mama on the phone and told her that I probably had leprosy and she and my father had three days to get me to the hospital in Honolulu.

When we got home, Mama and Dad were there and when they saw me they both began to cry. The nurse talked to them for a little while and they nodded and cried more. I stood there, but I didn't understand anything they said. I didn't feel sick any more.

The nurse left. My parents were still crying. They asked me to forgive them and to please not hold anything against them.

"Okay," I said. But until now I had never heard the world "leprosy" and I had no idea what I was forgiving them for. Later that afternoon my brothers Joseph and David came home and the whole family talked about me. The next day Mama got out the *paiki*—a suitcase—and put my things in it.

"Where are we going?" I asked.

"Never mind," she said, putting in the hated pair of shoes. She packed enough, it seemed to me, to stay a month.

On Wednesday morning, in the middle of the night really, my Dad loaded the suitcases on the car, a black '34 Buick. My two brothers said good-bye to me in the parlor. They both cried, big as they were. But I didn't. I was the only one who didn't know what was going on.

It was not long after midnight when we pulled out of the garage and were off. I slept on the way because I thought we were headed for Kona, and for me, that was fine. I knew it was going to be a long ride from Ninole.

About 5:30 a.m., when it was getting to be daybreak, we came to a pier. This wasn't Kona, but the harbor at Kawaihae. Nearby was a corral, store and gas station. That was all. Dad stopped and he and Mom took a nap in the car.

I got out and went to look around. Inside a warehouse on the wharf a cowboy lay asleep with his saddle under his head for a pillow and his horse blanket over him. I said to myself, "This place dead."

But soon I saw cowboys driving cattle down the hillside, right into the corral. Wow! Cowboys! Just like in the movies, but these cowboys were real. They had real cowboy hats, and red neckerchiefs! I found out they never used a truck. They rode their horses all the way from the ranch, driving the cattle.

There must have been a hundred cows in the corral, all mooing. They were packed so close, I couldn't count them. I liked the way the cowboys worked their horses. I had only ridden once, and it was just that mule back in first grade.

When the cows were all corralled, the cowboys went into the ocean and washed themselves when they were done—clothes and all!

Pretty soon, over the horizon I could see a ship approaching. It anchored outside, and two small whaling boats came into the shallow water. Next thing I knew the cowboys were roping the mooing cattle out of the corral and pulling them out to the whaleboats where they tied them up against the gunwales. I could still hear them mooing. When they had six of them tied, sailors rowed the boat back to the ship. Then the cattle were lifted aboard into the bow of the ship. Each trip took about a half hour.

All of a sudden it was time for Mama and me to board one of the whale-boats. My father gave me a whole dollar and told me I could spend it in Honolulu on whatever I wanted. Then Mama and I climbed down a ladder from the pier into the boat, to be rowed to the waiting ship.

As we pulled away from shore I watched my Dad standing on the wharf crying. I had never seen him cry until the day the nurse came to our house with me. Now he wept hard enough to make the tide rise twice as high as it was. But why? We would be back in a few days. I know now that I was the only one who still thought so.

Mama waved to him. I waved, watching him crying and waving as he got smaller and smaller. By the time the boat got to the ship, the USS *Humuʻula*, I could barely see him at all.

We went up the ladder and onto the steerage deck, where we waited for the ship to pull anchor. I was excited about this trip, only my third time on a ship. But I looked back at the tiny dot that was my Dad and I cried. Mama was still crying. When the *Humuʻula* weighed anchor, Mama took the bandana from around her neck and waved it at my Dad. All of a sudden my heart felt like I wouldn't see him again for a long time.

Sailing was smooth at first, but as we got out into deeper water it began to get rough, the *Humuʻula*'s bow plowing into the oncoming swells. It would be a long trip from Kawaihae with many hours at sea. With nothing to do in steerage, we just watched as the ship pitched and rolled against the waves. I had the run of the boat and I took advantage of it, zipping up and down ladders and stairs from bow to stern, from port to starboard. I went to see the cattle in the bow, and I watched the *selamoku*, the sailors. They were rugged guys who knew their jobs and were not afraid. But in my book they were a cut below the cowboys.

Early that evening we pulled into Hana on Maui to pick up more cattle and freight, then slept the night on the deck. The ship did the same at Kaunakakai on Molokaʻi, where a man got on. That made three of us in steerage. We spent another night sleeping on mattresses on the deck, but I didn't see the man. Finally we went on to Honolulu on the island of Oʻahu, where we arrived so early on Friday morning it was still dark.

I hadn't seen the other passenger at all, but as soon as the gangplank was dropped, he hurried off the ship. Hardly anyone except Rachel was at the pier. She took the trolley with us downtown, where we all went to a small hotel at Beretania Street and Tin Pan Alley. We took a room there, two beds, a table and one chair, with a public bath down the hall. Mama and I shared one of the beds. We had a short nap and headed for breakfast at about 7:45 a.m.

Mama said we had to go to Dr. Chung-Hoon again. So we caught my favorite, the trolley car. I really didn't know where I was or why, but I was safe with Mama. I asked her where the other passenger on the ship had gone, but she didn't know.

Dr. Chung-Hoon examined me head to toe, back and front. When he finished we went back to our hotel room. Mama laid down to rest. I told her I was going downstairs to look around and she said not to go too far. She gave me a dollar and I went down to the street rich, with her dollar and the one my father had given me.

At a candy store, I asked, "How much ice cream?"

"Five cents one."

I think I didn't know how to count change, so I spent one whole dollar on ice cream. I bought 20 vanilla and chocolate Dixie cups and ate about 6 of the chocolate ones. What was left I took back upstairs to the hotel room. When Mama woke up she saw the wet package and asked what it was. I told her it was a dollar's worth of ice cream.

"We'll be eating that thing forever," she said. And she was almost right! She ate about six cups of vanilla, I ate most of the other chocolate cups, and the rest melted into a puddle.

Sunday we took the Waikīkī trolley. At Sans Souci beach I swam for the first time in the ocean. What's wrong with the water, I wondered. It's so salty, not like Jackson Pond in Nīnole where I learned to swim by jumping in.

I played with other kids. Mama sat on the beach, yelling at me not to go in too deep. She thought above my waist was too far. We returned to the hotel room, took a shower, and then went out for supper. We got back about 7 p.m. Mama looked at me sadly and began to cry. She held me against her and cried and cried. What was wrong? Had I done something bad? She didn't answer, just held me and cried. I asked her again.

"It's nothing you did," she sobbed. "It's where you have to go tomorrow.

I will never see you again."

"Why?"

"I wish your father was here," she cried. "I wish he was here."

It made me cry. I cried and held her, feeling that after tomorrow my life would never be the same. I didn't know why I felt that way, but I turned out to be right.

Monday afternoon we took a taxi, arriving at a gate where a sign said "Kalihi Receiving Station." We entered, and a man came up to our taxi.

"Who do you wish to see?"

"Either the doctor or the nurse," Mama said.

He told us to wait. He left, then returned with another person. She said her name was Mrs. Gonzalves and that she was the Head Nurse. "I am Mrs. Nalaielua," Mama said. "I have brought my son to be admitted."

The nurse opened the taxi door and told me to get out and bring my things.

She then turned to Mama. "I'm sorry, but you cannot come with your son. You must say good-bye now and leave the grounds."

The nurse led me away. I was too scared to look anywhere but straight ahead. If anyone could look back, they would be braver than I was. No one had told me anything much, least of all the truth. If I had known what was going to happen, it would have been easier. But I had not even been given a chance to ask where I was going. It was just cold turkey, with a stranger grabbing my arm. All I knew for sure was that my mother was crying and that her heart was breaking.

The day was May 12, 1936. I was ten years old. From this day, I would be forever known as a "leper."

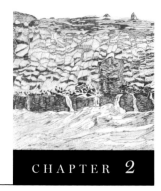

Kalihi Hospital

CHAPTER 2

Honolulu 1936

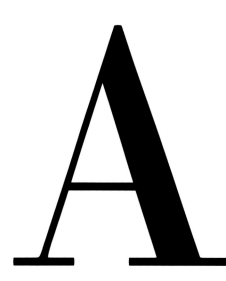

At Kalihi Hospital, for only the second time in my life, I had my supper in bed. Wow! Then I noticed that everyone in the other twelve beds, men, and some boys my age or a little older, were being served in bed too.

The three boys jibber-jabbered, asking all kinds of questions, trying to provoke me into doing something wrong, trying to put the newcomer in his place. I'd never been confronted that way, but I wasn't ready to run. I knew that if you fight, you lose. I didn't get cocky, but I thought, "If they beat me up, when I grow up I'll take them one by one."

It was 4:30 p.m. and I tried to eat my supper. I'd never had pork chops before. I decided they were my favorite. At 7:30 we were served a snack, hot or cold chocolate, or lemonade. They also gave us sandwiches so tiny you'd have to eat 20 to be satisfied.

About then I saw the man who had been with Mama and me on the boat! He was in the same place I was! He didn't see me, so I went over to him. When I got close, I found out I knew him from before! He had worked under my father, and he knew me because he used to come and clean our yard. He had kept to himself because he knew where we were going.

After about six weeks of doctors and nurses testing on my body, they told me someone would come to pick me up so I could go home. I packed my one suitcase, but I was too impatient to wait for the pickup. I remembered the way I had come into Kalihi Hospital and I followed that path to get out. I knew the gate was open from 4:30 a.m. to 9 p.m.

As soon as I passed through the gate, the adult patient sitting there, Sonny, yelled, "Hey, you! Where the hell do you think you're going?"

"Home," I said. "The nurses said I could go home." I kept walking.

"Wait!" Sonny hollered. "You're going the wrong way!" He ran up to me and grabbed my suitcase. "Hold it! You're going the wrong way. Follow me."

I did. He pointed me to a building in the distance. "See that big house over there?"

"Yeah."

"That's your home."

Someone else came up to me and said, "Ah! There you are! Let me take you home."

"That's not my home!" I was getting panicked.

"Follow me," the man said.

I did, looking back at the gate I knew would really take me home.

He led me through the front door of the building, where I saw a huge room filled with beds.

A woman met me. "My name is Mrs. Sphan. For now, there's your bed. Make yourself at home. You'll get to know everyone as time goes by. Don't worry about it. You'll meet them all. Remember that my name is Mrs. Sphan, and I'm your mother."

She told me how lucky I was to be here for treatment. I knew she was not my mother. And I began to notice a lot of things that didn't seem so lucky to me. In time I learned all this:

1. You can't leave the compound or hospital unless a doctor orders it.

2. You have no choice of quarters or room.

3. You cannot eat before the bell rings.

4. You can't be out of your building after 9 p.m. They called it 0900 hours. The youngest patients must be in bed by 8 p.m. You could read or listen to the radio, but you'd better be asleep by 9.

5. Adults must be in bed by 10 p.m.

6. You cannot refuse any treatment the doctor recommends.

7. You cannot touch, hug or kiss your family when they visit because you are separated by a fence.

8. You can receive stuff from them, but cannot give them anything that is not regulated and approved by the authorities.

9. You cannot enter some rooms in the compound without permission.

Never once in the five years I stayed at Kalihi did I enter the office of any doctor or even the Head Nurse. Not that I wasn't examined. What the doctors and nurses did was called "Progress." It happened in the staff building between 8:30 and 11 a.m. once a month. Even if it had happened only once in a lifetime, it would be unforgettable. I could multiply "unforgettable" by months that stretched over five years.

We waited our turns in a slew of cubicles, men first, then boys. After that, women, and last, girls. Nobody told me why we were there. Nobody asked if we wanted to do this. It was just the rule. Sometimes someone tried to refuse. His punishment was not being allowed to attend the movies or any recreational activities. It was a long time before I discovered that trouble makers who repeatedly tried to refuse "Progress" were sent to Kalaupapa.

I remember waiting naked in my cubicle. It was like a small closet, or a stall shower. I talked through the curtain to the kids on either side of me. What was I doing, standing naked in this stall?

Someone called out: "Next!"

I looked out the curtain and saw all these doctors and one nurse. The ten feet to the pedestal in the "Progress" room seemed like a mile. I was naked and I was cold. I was shame.

A doctor ordered me up a couple of steps to the top of the pedestal. It was round, like a barrel, and it turned. I stood on it, shifting from one foot to the other. I wanted my clothes. I wanted Mama. I wanted to run away from "Progress."

The doctor took up a long pointer, the kind teachers use at a blackboard. He held it in both hands and said, "This is Patient Number 3367."

That was my number. It is still my number.

The doctors and the nurse had lots of clothes on. The doctor pointed to things on my body, a patch or a blotch or a marking. A lesion, ulcer or open sore. And he did all the talking, in doctor's language.

He turned me on the pedestal, and the other doctors encircled it, asking questions. The chief doctor told me to look away. Then he tested my reaction to heat and cold. To see what I could feel, he touched me with a feather, and cotton, and pricked me with a needle.

It lasted 10 or 15 minutes. It felt like hours. It would happen again in a month, when the doctors would once again look for progress.

It took me a few years to realize that this was all a study for the doctors. It wasn't for us. But it only took me a time or two to hate the degrading, humiliating, shaming "Progress," where I was stared at, poked and prodded, like a bug you then step on.

"Progress" happened like clockwork to every one of the 75 or 100 patients. The doctors said it was to watch for enough progress that we could go home. Sometimes people went to the Observation Unit as another way toward discharge, but they could stay there ten years or more. Their chances of going home might be good but, if they went, chances were also good that they would come back.

For many years, I didn't realize that Federal and Territorial laws of the time, as well as the policies of the Hawai'i Board of Health and the procedures of the hospital, violated our human rights. We were denied the right to question our medication, even to ask if it had negative side effects, or what it was expected to accomplish.

With the other rules, daily life at Kalihi came down to incarceration, a life sentence with no prospect for parole. It was a death sentence too, because you would carry the stigma of the disease until the day you died. No matter what, you would always be known as a "leper."

The place looked like a prison too. An eight foot high chain-link fence with barbed wire at the top encircled the whole compound of just over 11 acres, keeping us in and everyone else out.

Yet there were a few bright spots. One of the best happened on Monday and Saturday evenings: movies. No matter how old or young anybody was, this was the one thing they looked forward to. We youngsters loved the weekly serials, relishing chapter after chapter. Our heroes were the stars of the Westerns, the rugged and tough guys who came on strong—Buck Jones, Wild Bill Elliott, Tom Mix, Hopalong Cassidy, Lash LaRue, Johnny Mack Brown, Gene Autry. Each kid had his favorite. Sometimes it was Tarzan, or Flash Gordon. Even the 75 yard walk to the theater was a good part of movie night, a time for friendship and sharing. It took our thoughts away from family and home for awhile. The "theater" was actually an all-purpose gym, with a pool table and badminton court. The projection room was way up a ladder and the movie reels were raised and lowered with a rope.

The gym theater didn't offer treats, but we could buy candy or ice cream from Asagi Store about 20 yards across the road from the hospital's main gate.

That little food store was precious. The Territorial government gave us each an allowance of five dollars a month, and some patients also earned spending money doing jobs at the hospital. For five cents we could buy a Butterfinger, Baby Ruth or Milky Way. Saimin cost 50 cents. Asagi Store had ice cream—I always bought chocolate—and shave ice too, and pastries. It opened every day from six in the morning until nine at night, and either Mr. or Mrs. Asagi, or their high school-age son Peter, was always within hearing distance.

"Asagi-san!" we'd yell out, and pretty soon one of them would walk up to the "caller line" and take our order. Sometimes they wrote it down on a pad. They could hand us our treats directly. But exchanging money was much more complicated.

Our money went into a small metal cashbox with a slot in the top and a padlock on the bottom. It was bolted to a post inside the fence, facing the store, so Asagi-san could see it. Every night a patient worker would disinfect the coins and bills with alcohol.

"Why do you do that?" I asked.

"You don't have to know," the worker said. "You're too young."

I asked Asagi-san.

"They have to do that to the money, or we wouldn't be allowed to sell you things." He told me the alcohol would kill leprosy germs on the coins and currency. Much later I found out that at the time, doctors still didn't know what caused leprosy or how it was spread. Like all the other treatments and precautions up to that point, the alcohol was a stab in the dark.

We liked being able to buy treats from Asagi-san. But three of my friends and I also schemed to steal the money box. Our plan was short-lived. We were trying to figure out how we would get the money out of the box when another kid put the fear in us: Somebody would big mouth and it would be the end. Asagi-san wouldn't want us as customers anymore and we would have to run away to go to the store. We gave up our idea.

Going to Mass didn't do much to turn me into a totally good boy, but Bishop Alencastre came every Sunday, rain or shine. Nobody asked us Catholic kids if we wanted to go, they just said go. I liked the sound of Latin, soft, like Hawaiian. I learned my catechism and was confirmed.

Another thing that happened for the good was that I started playing music with a bunch of guys. I particularly remember Charles Ka'ai and David Hewahewa. I borrowed a 'ukulele. It came easily to me.

When I was three months short of my twelfth birthday, the doctor told me I was sick, having a "reaction" to leprosy. This kind of inflammatory complication usually starts with a high fever up to 105 degrees. Then come chills, weakness in the arms and legs, even paralysis in the face and hands, swelling below the biceps. Sometimes red lesions cover more than half of the body, like little islands on your skin with reddish/white markings. All of the skin becomes numb to the touch of a feather or the prick of a pin, or to hot or cold water. The symptoms can last anywhere from a month to a year.

I was sick, flat on my back in a hospital bed, and the rest of the world was going by. I had to have help from a nurse or orderly just to sit up in bed. I had to use a bedpan. To get around anywhere, to go to the bathroom or to physical therapy, I had to have an orderly push me in a wheelchair. No matter how hard I tried, when I touched something I could not feel it. I couldn't feel anything in my legs either. It was like my body was making a transfer without my permission. I was nestled under a thing the nurses called "the doghouse." It was kind of like an igloo made of wire and covered with a sheet or blanket. It fit over me from the chest down and had a lightbulb in it to make me warm.

But sometimes I was too hot, fevered with sweat, and then went into a cold sweat and spasms. The sweat soaked me so badly, the nurses sometimes changed my pajamas four or five times a day.

My mind went into complete panic. I grew more afraid by the minute, terrified I wouldn't see another day. Would I ever see Mama again? Or my father and my brothers? I was too weak to think, and I cried a lot from pain. I could almost see my life passing in the eyes of the nurses, orderlies, doctors, and even the janitors. They all gave extra care, constantly checking my temperature and blood pressure, giving me hot and cold soaks, making me take pills and drink water. They would bring my tray at mealtime, but I had no interest in food and no strength to eat anyway. They'd come back in 15 minutes. My food would still be there, and they'd force it down my throat. I hated almost all vegetables and fruit, especially brussels sprouts, broccoli and asparagus. Meatloaf was my enemy. The only thing I liked was lettuce and tomato. And breakfast—cocoa, toast, waffle, hotcake, eggs and bacon.

The only really good thing was sleeping a lot, an escape from being despondent.

I didn't have to go to "Progress," but it came to me. A group of doctors would come by my bed and the head doctor would lecture them: "Now this is a typical reaction . . ."

After some months, the reaction began to subside. My fever was almost gone. My skin took on better color, the patches of lesions slowly disappeared. I was weak and skinny, but my appetite became voracious and I started picking up weight.

After three months in a bed with occasional short trips in a wheelchair and practicing with a walker, I took my first step alone without a nurse or an aide.

The nurses and orderlies and my friends in the other beds called encouragement.

"Come on, Henry! You can make it!"

I smiled. This was good!

Soon I could walk to the bathroom. Finally I got to take a shower, after months of nurses giving me sponge baths in bed, scrubbing me down on a rubber sheet. I stayed in the shower almost half an hour, yelling my head off from happiness.

After six or seven months going to hell and back, everything was looking up. I had another chance at life! I remember the nurses. Miss Tanaka, Miss Fujioka, Mrs. Keala, and the head nurse, Mrs. Gonzalves. Also Mrs. Brian and Mrs. Seveneck. I liked them. One of the nurses said, "You're nice and strong now. There was a time when we were going to lose you."

What?! The doctors don't tell you that you're near death, but everybody knows, except you and your parents. They don't tell your family unless you die.

I kept asking the doctor, "When I going be discharged?"

He kept avoiding an answer. Eventually I did learn some patience. And eventually he did discharge me. Now I thank God and the doctors, nurses, orderlies, and everybody else who helped in restoring my health. I'm even thankful for the experimenting with therapy and medication.

It was now May, 1938. Not only was I 12 now, but while I was in the hospital, I had grown several inches. It was strange to see how much my friends had grown too. It was almost time for summer vacation and I was the happiest boy alive. I was back in the Boys' Building with nine other boys and the "housefather" or "patron." I remember Frank and his brother Danny, and another Danny. Outside, we chased each other, and played a little baseball. We didn't have enough kids for a team, but three or four of us would pitch and bat, or we'd throw a football.

The elders would sit outside on the veranda of their buildings talking story about the good and bad events of the day. Sometimes they warmed up food in a pot on an electric hotplate and we got a chance to eat with them. We kids didn't have cooking utensils for ourselves. I think the doctors discouraged cooking to keep patients from getting burned. I got out of the hospital just in time to be part of the new program for teenagers, the taking of cod liver oil. Most of the boys I knew would hold it in their mouths until they could get away from the nurse, and then they spit it out. But I liked it. Sometimes I drank doses that were meant for other kids. The nurses offered us orange bits to take away the taste of the cod liver oil, but I never took any orange pieces. The cod liver oil helped me gain weight and brought color to my skin.

By the end of the year, I was really back to normal. And my status had changed. I was 13 now, a young man. I was moved from the Boys' Building dormitory to Makalapua, a residence for ten adult and young men. Our housefather was a patient named Aki Wong. Everybody liked him. Our rooms were on one side of a long, one-story building, opening onto a veranda. The bathroom was in the middle section that joined Makalapua to a women's residence, Ho'ikeana.

Now I had my own room. Each room had a bed, table, chair and closet. Some had a chiffonier or a bureau. The light hung from the ceiling on a drop cord. We could stay out an hour longer, until 9 p.m., and had to be in bed by 9:30 or 10. A bell system would tell us what time it was, starting at 6 p.m. When you heard the last bell at 10 p.m. everyone was supposed to be at home or in bed with nobody walking around the compound.

I was now enjoying this new life away from all the younger boys, on my own with the older men. We played touch football and volleyball, and shot baskets. Sometimes we had enough guys for a basketball team. Some men moved to the residence called Hawai'i Pono'i and others went to Oriental Building within the compound. That made room for more boys to move to Makalapua. The older girls moved from Ho'ikeana to Mothers' Building.

Hardly anyone moved to Horseshoe Terrace, which had some hospital beds and was used primarily for the mentally ill.

I soon discovered something worse than "Progress." It came around once or twice a year in the theater. It was actually called The Monkey Show.

We patients were the monkeys, on the stage. The men and boys wore only their shorts. Women and girls wore bra and panties under a hospital gown open in the back.

Any number of people were in the audience, all training to be doctors, nurses or physical therapists. The presiding doctor used the "Progress" pointer to give his lecture. He paraded us across the stage, calling us out one by one.

"Next!" he'd shout. Or "Next group!" He never said anyone's name or even his or her number.

He called me. I was to stand in the middle of the stage and turn on cue as the doctor gave an oral medical history of my illness. He pointed to my various nodules or scars or other symptoms, lecturing about these as if I weren't even there. It would have been better to be a real monkey.

All I got for being in The Monkey Show was a cup of chocolate ice cream. While I ate it, I thought, "When I get old enough, I'll tell them all to go to hell."

Even after The Monkey Show, we still had to go to the monthly "Progress" in the doctor's building. One day, while I was in my "Progress" cubicle waiting to be called, a kindly old Chinese man called me to his cubicle.

I was a little scared, but curious, and I watched as he did something I'd never seen before. I stared at his crippled hands as he drew something on a paper with a pen and black India ink. He had different points for the pen. When he finished the drawing, he began to color it with crayons.

"Wow," I said, "You can do a lot of stuff. Can you teach me?"

"This is called calligraphy," he said. He told me his name was Joseph Leong, and that he would teach me. But he also said, "I want you to do something for me."

"Anything you want," I said.

"Do you want to become a Boy Scout?"

"Yeah! You bet!"

After that I started seeing Mr. Leong often. With his crippled hands he could do calligraphy and crayon painting and tie all kinds of knots. He was a humble, soft spoken Chinese man who worked his best within his physical limits and who excelled with his mind. For me, he also symbolized truth, honesty and reverence.

I knew next to nothing about Scouting. How would I get a uniform? I had no money. Mr. Leong told me not to worry about the money.

But I did, and it made me think about home too. My eyes filled with tears wondering about my family. I was glad I was alone in my room. I lay down on the bed and cried into my pillow. I had never asked my parents for money. If Dad sent me any it was because he wanted to, not because I asked. As I lay there with all these thoughts in my head, somehow a uniform came. I don't know how.

Later that day I saw Mr. Leong.

He said, "You have your uniform?"

"Yes."

"How does it fit?"

"It fits," I said.

We were Boy Scout Troop no. 46. Another adult man in our troop, our school teacher, Albert Like, was Scoutmaster, along with Mr. Leong. He was small, like Mr. Leong, and similar in mental stature. His hands were crippled, and also his feet. But he was always ready for questions no matter what, and made up in wisdom what he lacked in physical capacity. He reminded me of Solomon in the Bible. To me, he and Mr. Leong were two of the smartest and wisest people I have ever known.

Some regular Scouting things we couldn't do. We tried the 14-mile hike by walking across the compound grass, back and forth, up and down. It was boring and monotonous. We did the fundamentals, like learning to type, and to make a two-match fire. First aid was kind of pointless. After all, we were already in a hospital. Why worry about it?

One day Mr. Leong held up a bar of soap. "What is this for?"

"Bathe."

"No," he said. "To make water boil faster." He put it in a pot of water on a stove. I thought it was stupid. I come from a place where you cook outside. Aunties and Uncles come over and you cook one big pot of stew on the open fire. You're not going to put soap in everything you cook.

Mr. Leong helped us with artwork, using crayons and watercolors. I had been doodling since I was four, and I enjoyed this. When he found I could really draw, he took me aside and showed me more techniques. I learned how to blend colors with crayons, and to draw and paint in perspective. Later, when he was bedridden in the hospital, I'd visit him and we'd work on art.

Mr. Leong knew a lot of things. He was a history buff, and sometimes he'd talk about the Romans.

"Who the hell are the Romans?" I had no idea.

He talked about Julius Caesar and Augustus.

I said, "Who?"

He talked about people like Hercules, and Samson. He was a good player at checkers and chess, but I wasn't interested in that, only in doing creative things with my hands.

One time the Governor of the Territory came to visit Kalihi Hospital. Governor Poindexter inspected Boy Scout Troop No. 46. What an honor!

But it was not enough to keep me in Boy Scouts. After awhile, to my friends and me, anything having to do with being good, doing good, or being nice didn't seem fun. I quit Boy Scouts. My friends and I decided we'd rather work and earn money instead of going to school. Our classes started at 8 a.m. and we'd go in about 9. This was our way of rebelling against the system that had taken away our freedom.

We didn't study and the teacher couldn't force us. To me, studying was as bad as meatloaf.

I liked the morning breaks in the school day. At the first one, we got the cod liver oil. At the second, we could use shops tools—skill saw, drill, coping saw, files, sandpaper. I liked it, and it took me away from the school lessons.

But all of it was pointless. If people were so educated and smart, how come I didn't see anybody going out the gate?

When I was 14, I moved again, to Hawai'i Pono'i. Several men had moved out and their rooms were vacant. I found out they had gone to somewhere called Kalaupapa. I remembered sometimes seeing patients departing from the hospital at 5 a.m. I thought they were going home. But they were being taken to a pier to catch a boat to Kalaupapa. I would find out more about this later.

But at the moment, I was bored. So were my friends. Some played music. I borrowed an 'ukulele and joined Charles Ka'ai, Herbert, and David Hewahewa. It felt good to play some music. But it wasn't enough. Some of us began to think about what might lie beyond the fence.

A holiday was coming up Friday, and the escape team went into high gear planning. Sam Kama, an older boy, had been going over the fence. And he talked about it. If he could, so could we!

A lot of guys besides Sam had run, and there was already a hole under the fence at the Ewa corner. The last escapee had covered it with dry grass. If you weren't looking for it, you wouldn't see it. But we saw it. It would be better than going over the top, with the barbed wire.

We formed our plan, John Keola, Danny and Frank Kekahuna, Joe Kaihe, Peter Reed, Dennis and I—and Sam Kama—all from Hawai'i Pono'i.

One kid—a different kid each time we planned an escape—told his relatives during visiting that morning, "We like run away tonight. We like you pick us up." So each time, it would be a different parent.

The plan for our first escape was to go to the bakery, and the movies. We'd leave about 6:30 or 7 p.m. In three or four hours, we'd come back, before the last bell.

Sam Kama, the "elder spokesman," who was 16 or 17, told us we would need fake ID in case a policeman questioned us about being out after the eight o'clock curfew. We made the ID by filling out the cards that come with a wallet. I wrote my age as 17.

Our leader told us to dress to look old—open collar, rolled up sleeves, pants with crease—but no rolled up pants. And think big, he said, like you 18 or over.

Finally we really went under the wire. We were free! Away we went in the arranged car. Our driver dropped us off at a pastry shop close to Farrington High School. My favorite thing was a longjohn, a rectangular doughnut with maple frosting. Next we went to the Palama Theater. I can't remember the name of the movie, but, of course, first we saw the newsreel and the cartoons. Admission was 25 cents. We also bought candies.

To come back, we were going to meet our ride at A'ala Park, but we were late. Our car had come and gone. We decided to walk back via Iwilei and the Kalihi district. After stealing some comic books and odds and ends, we ate at the Oahu Railway Cafe. About half way home, we walked the wrong way through a Kalihi neighborhood. From a yard, one of the hospital cooks saw us. We didn't look at her even though we knew she had caught us red-handed.

"Where you boys went?" she asked.

None of us answered. But we knew we'd hear about this in the morning.

And we did. About eight o'clock Ma Clinton, the hospital administrator, wanted us up at the main building. There were four of us who had got caught, Joe, Frank, Danny and myself. When Ma was *pau* (done) lecturing and scolding, she said, "For your punishment you'll each take a corner of this office, until I say you can leave. Otherwise you can only leave for meals."

"What if we have to go bat'room?"

"Only one of you at a time."

So we started a game, taking turns asking to go, one after the other, all day long. By the third round, she caught on. After that we could each go only three times a day, at different times. But when she wasn't in the room, we'd walk around, talk, sit on the table.

After two weeks she let us go, but only when we vowed never to run away again. If we did, she said, the punishment would be more severe—no movies for a month or two. We promised. We knew better now. We had learned our lesson. Which was where to travel to and from the hospital so as not to get caught.

Later I realized that Ma Clinton was a good woman. She really cared for the patients. At the time, she gave us a headache, but really, it was us who gave her the headache. She had to punish us because we were wrong, so we hated her. We knew we were wrong, but the thing was, older people didn't have the same punishment—and most people did go under the fence.

The watchmen let us escape, especially the big Hawaiian, Douglas Kekina. Actually, he owed us. He liked to drink on his shift, and when he did, he would forget to ring the bell that announced the hour. He'd ring it six times when he started his shift at 6 p.m., and maybe at 7 p.m. but later he'd forget. We'd ring it for him.

"What! You guys going?" he would say. "Go, so long you bring me back pastry."

I made my fourth escape with Dan Kekahuna. Our ride dropped us off in town where we wanted to go. Men knew about this Hotel Street district, but not boys.

We'd heard all about these places from an adult patient who—it was told on the grapevine—had been busted as a small-time racketeer and spent time in the "Big House." When he contracted leprosy, he was sent from prison to Kalihi Hospital. He volunteered to go to Kalaupapa. He did, but was later indicted for murder, convicted, and sent back to prison, where, we thought, he was killed.

Before any of that happened, he gave us the lowdown on all these places—about four on Hotel Street, two on A'ala Park Lane, and some down on Iwilei Road.

The Rex Rooms on Smith Street was the easiest to find.

I followed Danny up an inside stairway to the second floor. We walked in. Here and there were pictures of naked women in various poses. We could see rooms on both sides of a hallway.

As we stood in the doorway, a woman looked at us both and then said to me, "Boy, they are getting younger and younger."

I said, "You like see my ID?"

"I believe I do," she said.

I got so nervous I could barely get it out of my pocket.

"Never mind," she said. "I'll take your word for it. When were you born?"

"Uh, uh, November third, uh, uh . . ." I almost blew it. She started to laugh. Before I could say more, she looked at me and at the card in my hand.

"I'm going to give you a break. Come on in and wait until someone comes for you."

After awhile a couple of men left. Two curtains parted slightly and a woman beckoned to me. I went over to her, and behind those curtains she turned me into a young man.

Over a long period of time, I went back to the Rex Rooms twice with the guys, but I decided I couldn't part with my hard-earned money that way. But I still went under the fence.

We got so we timed the watchman's routine so we could march right through the front gate. We acted like we lived outside instead of in the hospital.

Once we walked a couple of blocks to a school yard, where we saw several people but didn't approach them. Suddenly Raymond spotted his older brother coming toward us.

"Eh, we gotta go back," Raymond said. "That's my brother and I know he saw me."

We started back to the hospital on the double, sliding under the fence and into our building before anyone saw us.

At 6:30 the next morning someone came to call Raymond because he had a visitor. As Raymond walked up the caller line, he saw that the person was his brother. He raked Raymond over the coals. When Raymond came back he was laughing, but only because his brother couldn't touch him.

After breakfast we decided it was time to be more careful whenever we left the compound.

One Friday about 4 p.m. Frank, Joe and I were sitting on our porch at Hawai'i Pono'i when we saw the night watchman, Douglas Kekina. One look at him told us he was drunk. He asked us for an empty room where he could sleep it off until he came on duty at 6. We showed him the room, and he just sprawled out on the bare mattress and was asleep instantly. About 5:00 or 5:30 he woke up but was still too drunk to go to work. We told Kekina not to worry. We would do his watch for him, ringing the bell until ten o'clock. He went back to bed. So we watched the compound for any trouble or anything suspicious. All went well and about 11:30 Kekina got up and finished his shift.

Saturday back he came, drunk again. This time he brought us some cold milk, some of it chocolate, maybe as a bribe to help him. Again we watched for him. Sunday night came and we wanted out, even if only for a short time. Kekina was reasonably sober, enough to do his work, so five of us went under the fence about seven o'clock, to the movies at Palama Theater. We saw *The Champ* starring Wayne Morris. Afterwards we bought pastries at the bakery before returning. Kekina was waiting for us in a corner right outside our building.

"What the hell took you guys so long?" he growled. "I been waiting for hours." He made it such a big deal that we were stunned. Then he laughed. "Let's go get some coffee and milk to go with the goodies."

After that whenever he was on duty, we went under.

It was the perfect set-up. But then Mr. Yee, a carpenter who doubled as night watchman, put a kink in our style. He had a hunch whenever we planned to go under the fence, and started sneaking around our building. This went on for two or three weeks.

We'd split the group so he'd always see some of us and think all of us were home. We left the lights on in one or two rooms, and sometimes we played the radio too. One night everyone left except for me. I was in my room in the dark, but lights were on in two other rooms.

After the ten o'clock bell, Mr. Yee made his rounds. Passing our building, he saw the light on but it must have seemed too quiet. From my darkened room I watched him open doors. No one was in the rooms. He knew then the lights were a decoy. Once he opened my door and found me sleeping. He went to sit on the porch. When he had to make hourly rounds he would do it fast, then come back and sit, waiting.

About 10:30 the gang came home. They saw Mr. Yee on the porch before he could see them. Some of the rooms opened onto the other side of the building. They dropped the pastries in one of these, then went to sneak through another room. But Mr. Yee knew. He went to the room with the pastries, sat down, ate his fill, and took the rest with him.

When the boys returned, they found nothing but crumbs. About eight the next morning, as Mr. Yee came by Hawai'i Pono'i, they walked towards him. He knew this was a show down and he tried to walk away, but the boys surrounded him.

"Why you went take our pastries?"

"I nevah eat you guys' pastries," he said.

The circle of boys got tighter. "Yeah, so how come all gone den?"

We waited, and looked at him. "Eh, 'cause you guys went make me look like one damfool bugga."

They still surrounded him, starting to get mean, demanding their money back. I could tell Mr. Yee was getting scared.

"Try wait," he said. "I let you guys go whenever you like go." He kept repeating it, until it soaked in. And when he came on duty the next night, Mr. Yee brought us pastries.

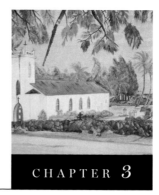

Kalaupapa

CHAPTER 3

Moloka'i 1941

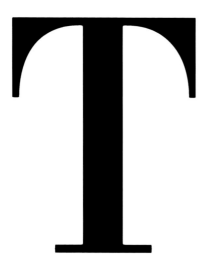

The matter of the pastries was settled, but in the eyes of the administration, we had escaped too often. We got the ultimate punishment meted out to patients the staff could not control. In the summer of 1941 we received letters telling us we'd be leaving with the September shipment to Kalaupapa. Shipment, that's what they said. We were just like cattle. A boat went twice a year, but it was mid-June already, too late for the first trip.

I wrote to my parents, telling them the time had come for me to move on to a new place and a new life. Sometime that summer, my family came to Honolulu. My father and mother came the first day, and my two brothers the following day. Then my parents came three days straight, trying to figure a way to hold me back. My father knew no one ever returned from Kalaupapa, but he still hoped that some day I'd be able to come home from Kalihi Hospital.

One day he said, "You must have run away."

"Yeah," I said.

"How many times?" He was looking right at me, his lousy son.

"Ho," I said. "Too much." Lucky I was inside the fence. Otherwise he would have beat me up.

"Don't you have a watchman?"

"Yeah. They cannot watch us all day." Then I added, "If you hold me back here, I'll run away again."

"You tell me why you run," he demanded.

"I like go Kalaupapa."

"Your two sisters went there." He sounded desperate. "And they died."

I had already found that out at Kalihi Hospital, but I didn't say a thing.

After that, on the fourth day, he gave up. I didn't see him and my mother again until I was paroled in 1949. Paroled, that's what they called it. Just like from prison.

After we got our letters, we tried to live our normal lives. School was closed for the summer, but we worked at our regular jobs. I was a janitor and a yard man. In the evenings we played sports or mah-jongg, always making sure we were seen often. But our trips under the fence became more and more frequent. If we got caught, so what? I got paid cash for my work and I spent it all on our illegal outings.

Suddenly September came. What do we pack? The bureau? The table?

"I going take my chair," I said to Sam Kama, our house patron, as defiant as I had been with my father.

"Why you do that?"

"Because I like."

In the end, I borrowed a suitcase and took only my clothes and shoes. I didn't even save any of my drawings.

Sunday we talked about the trip itself. Are we heading for paradise or hell? Some guys were on edge. Monday, September 21, was the longest day. All of us were packed and we had nothing to do but wait. Night came, and I had a hard time falling asleep. Even though I had said I wanted to go, now the old terror of uncertainty came to my mind. Would the ocean be rough?

How would we land? Who would meet us? Once again, no one had told us much. I didn't even know where Kalaupapa was!

Finally I did sleep. Then suddenly it was 4:30 a.m. Somehow we all managed to get up about the same time.

The watchman, George Rogers, told us, "Get your stuff out. They'll pick it up. Go to the main gate and wait there."

We put our bags on the sidewalk, like so much rubbish waiting to be picked up. We were served a little light breakfast while we waited. But what were we waiting for? We didn't know. Hawai'i Pono'i was empty. We had been the most troublesome bunch, and every last soul was going to Kalaupapa. The whole group included about 15 of us teenage boys, about 5 girls, and maybe 10 adult men and women.

Some people's families came to the gate, and the patients crowded on their side of the fence. I saw stolen kisses and secret handshakes, sometimes even when the guard was looking. Except for other patients staying behind, I didn't really have anyone to say good-bye to, and I thought, "When in the hell are we going to get away from here?"

Ma Clinton arrived about 5:30 a.m. She said a few words and "Good-bye" to everyone. A lot of patients came to say good-bye and hug us.

Two Army transport trucks rolled up. The side canvases were already down. We climbed in through the back and sat on benches along the sides. The Army guys rolled the back canvas down except for a space at the bottom. It was dark inside. Nobody outside was supposed to know we were in there. We were like a military secret. Some people started crying. Some tried to talk to their families, but they couldn't see them.

Our truck started up. When it started rolling, I looked back one last time through the small opening at the bottom of the back canvas. Everybody was waving.

When we arrived at the waterfront, it was still dark. The drivers backed to the pier and loaded our freight and then us directly from the trucks up the gangplank onto the stern of the SS *Hawai'i*. It was a cattle boat. We'd get off at the first stop at Kalaupapa and the cows would go on to other ports.

About 6 a.m., when the sky was beginning to get light, we pulled away from the pier at last. The ship carried us out through the harbor into the blue ocean offshore. We saw mountains, and then a stretch of sand we all thought was Waikīkī. We found out later that it was. I don't remember Diamond Head, but maybe we were too far out by then. As the view faded, the morning sun blazed with a new day. On we sailed, the ship bucking and pitching. Just as when I had traveled between islands before, I didn't get seasick, but most everyone else did.

As our sea journey continued, there came a vast emptiness of sky and water. Land seemed to be lost with time. Then, sometime later, we saw an island off the ship, to the right.

"Hey, there's Moloka'i!" someone called out.

I couldn't make it out, and neither could a lot of others, but we were curious, and kept looking hard as we sailed on. Finally we saw the island, and as we sailed, it got longer and more mountainous.

Then: "Hey! There it is, straight ahead!"

Kalaupapa is flat, but it slowly came into sight. All of a sudden time became important. Our journey would end soon.

As the sailors prepared to anchor, they told us to move from the port to the starboard deck. The ship slowed, gradually coming to a stop to anchor offshore and lower its two motor launches. We climbed down a rope ladder into the launches. I was in the first boat with about eight other passengers. By now I was excited at the thought of getting to see old friends again.

In about ten minutes we reached the wharf, stepped off the launch, and were led up cement stairs. A man called out our names, directing us where to gather.

"Henry Nalaielua!" he shouted. "Baldwin Home! Over there!" He pointed to a spot.

He called other names. "Bishop Home there! Bay View Home over here!" Then we waited for our boxes, suitcases and trunks. When they were unloaded from the launch, I grabbed mine off the pile.

"Eh, Henry!" It was Big Ed Kapilieha from Kalihi. We'd been in

Makalapua Building together, he and I and Frank Oka. Frank had died the year before at Kalihi. Eddie had gone to Kalaupapa about the time we started running away. By now he was about 17 or 18.

"How you?" I asked.

"We go," he said, pointing to a truck.

About ten of us—and Eddie—bound for Baldwin Home crowded into the bed of the truck and off we went, a small adult guy driving.

As we drove, I saw cowboys along the road. They wore neckerchiefs just like the paniolo (cowboys) I had seen five years ago when Mama and I had left Kawaihae on the cattle boat. I was amazed at what else I saw too. I thought, "Wow, this place big—roads, stores, churches, gas station, houses, cars! Just like New York!"

I also saw some people with ulcerated faces. I thought, "I never going look like that."

After a short ride, the truck drove through a gate and stopped in front of a wide building. Eddie gestured toward the entrance and said, "This Baldwin Home. I stay over here. You too, from now on."

I liked what I saw, especially when I found out I was assigned to room with Ed. Joe, Dan, and Dan's brother Frank were in the same dormitory. Eddie was the only old resident among us. Others lived in cottages nearby, but were still part of Baldwin Home. The main door opened from a porch into a hallway with a wing on each side. Each wing had two dorms, and in each dorm were six beds and six closets. By some of the beds were small tables. Our dorm faced the Baldwin Home gate, and beyond that we could see the ocean. I put my suitcase by my bed. It wasn't too long before someone rang a big handbell.

Eddie said, "Time for supper."

We went into the dining room in a building behind the dorms and connected by a breezeway. I was assigned to a rectangular table for six. One other guy besides me was new, and I also knew Eddie. We went to a counter to serve ourselves chop steak.

With the exception of one person, we all looked normal enough. Some of the boys who already lived at Baldwin Home wore the cowboy neckerchiefs. One of them at our table was smoking. But he never blew out any smoke! Instead, the smoke came from under the kerchief around his neck. I stared for a long time, but still couldn't understand how he did this.

"Eh, Henry," Eddie said. "No stare."

"I never see smoke come out a handkerchief before," I said.

I saw another man at a different table do the same thing.

They didn't seem to mind me staring. I asked Eddie, "How come they can do that?"

Eddie explained. Leprosy had made it impossible for some patients to breathe through their nostrils so they had had tracheotomies. The bandana covered the opening.

"What he get in his neck?" I asked.

"Tube," Eddie said.

"Like one tire tube?"

"Nah!" Eddie laughed. "Only small, like your finger maybe."

Before long, I realized that Kalaupapa was full of "cowboys."

A lot of guys at Baldwin Home had come from Kalihi Hospital with me—Charlie, Bill, Timothy, Tony, Sam, Awa, Wally, Robert, Minoru. An older boy who had come earlier was there too, Johnny Martin. They all had lived in Makalapua and Hawai'i Pono'i. Some of them were in the Boy Scouts with me.

I slept well that night, in my room with Eddie. The next morning I woke up early on my own and did the regular morning duties I'd learned at Kalihi, to fix my bed, wash my face, brush my teeth. I wandered outside, looking around. The mountains rose close behind Baldwin Home, tall, rugged, majestic. They fell straight into a very blue Pacific Ocean, and rolling surf kissed the shoreline. After Kalihi, the view and the place seemed especially beautiful.

After breakfast in the dining room at my regular table with the regular guys, Johnny Martin said, "Let's go riding!"

"Sure," I said. "Now."

He walked to a car, and away the two of us went. First we went through the Settlement, past Bay View and McVeigh Homes for single and married adults, and Bishop Home for single women and girls. The village itself also had stores, a recreation hall and churches. I was especially interested in the theater. Then we passed some graves, more ocean, and an area I couldn't figure out.

John said, "Airport." He saw me looking funny. "No more runway. The airplane land on the grass, slow down, stop at the terminal." He pointed. The "terminal" looked like a little house.

Farther on, a lighthouse loomed large. A white house stood nearby, with a red roof like the lighthouse. "Who live over there?" I asked.

"One married couple and their children. One boy and two girls."

I didn't see anyone, but the place looked lived in. Laundry flapped on the clotheslines. Hanging from a wire fence, a sign said in big, black letters, "U.S. COASTGUARD STATION. KEEP OUT. ENTER WITH PERMISSION ONLY."

We continued, with the deep blue ocean and pounding surf on one side. On the other the mountains were pointing straight up into the clouds. This land was bigger than I thought, although barren and rocky. Offshore, I saw two islets, but John didn't know their names. We came to a concrete platform with a tall derrick.

"Who use that?" I asked. "For what?"

"Same like the wharf at Kalaupapa," John said, "except this derrick only used if Kalaupapa too rough."

I pictured the boat we sailed on coming around this way, and the derrick hauling freight, and people coming ashore to get trucked to Kalaupapa. This steep, rocky place did not look like a hospitable landing spot.

We stopped at Siloama, a small church that looked in bad shape, its paint faded and its grounds so overgrown with lantana and *haole koa* that we couldn't go inside. Then we stopped at another church.

"This Damien's Church," John said. "Come inside."

"Who this buggah Damien?" I wondered. I had never heard of the famous priest, even though I was Catholic from birth. Inside it was moldy, and kind of stuffy too. To me it felt eerie, yet very calm and serene.

We passed a place with several tall concrete pillars.

"One hospital stay here before," John said. But that was all he knew. We started back by another route, passing mountains on our left. I thought the goats we saw were tame, but John said they were wild. They lived back in the valleys that cut into the mountains.

We got back to Baldwin Home a half hour before lunch. "What a morning," I thought. I felt lucky for the trip around Kalaupapa peninsula and all that I saw and learned.

After lunch Eddie and I talked. He told me about his life since I had last seen him in Kalihi several years before. We walked around Baldwin Home. He showed me the pig pen and the farm where one of the Catholic Brothers raised chickens, ducks and rabbits for Baldwin Home. Eddie showed me the banana farm and the papaya farm, all fruits to be distributed among Kalaupapa's other homes. Some separate cottages were part of Baldwin Home, and a workshop to clean chickens and ducks and grind ice cream. What a place to live. So much to learn! And learn I would from this place called Baldwin Home.

I would learn there were three other unit homes at Kalaupapa, but everybody I lived with thought Baldwin Home was the best. It housed about 40 of us. The place was the second Baldwin Home for boys and single young men, converted from the original Kalaupapa Hospital. The occupants moved there in 1932 when the new hospital was built. Before then, they had lived in the first Baldwin Home at Kalawao on the eastern side of the peninsula, where the whole Settlement used to be. This first Baldwin Home had been started in 1886 and was added to until it was a sprawling complex. When the residents moved in 1932, the buildings were torn down and the lumber salvaged. All that remains today are some stone fences and remnants of an oven.

When the order of Franciscan Sisters came to Kalaupapa in 1888 with Mother Marianne Cope, Bishop Home for girls and single women was built with funds from Charles Reed Bishop, a prominent banker and the husband of the late Bernice Pauahi Bishop, a high chiefess descended from Kamehameha. Later, the Territorial government built Bay View Home for about 60 single men, naming it for ʻAwahua Bay, which it overlooked. It comprised two cottages and two long buildings, with a general kitchen. A resident manager supervised it. McVeigh Home, farther inland, had about two dozen cottages for married couples and some apartments. About 90 patients lived in McVeigh, with a resident manager in a private cottage surrounded by a picket fence to make sure patients didn't intrude. At all the homes, the yards were immaculately clean. In addition to the general hospital, a 12-bed hospital for women was on the Bishop Home premises.

I would soon learn that, despite Bay View and McVeigh having far more residents than Baldwin Home, we had more able-bodied among us and were much more independent. In retrospect, I think some of our independence was our location away from the center of the Settlement, across Waihanau Stream.

One day I asked Eddie, "Eh, who that small kid?"

Eddie laughed. "He one old man!"

"Nah! The truck driver? That small shrimp? How he can reach the clutch?"

Eddie laughed again. Kenso Seki was not even five feet tall, but he was 25 or 30 years old. He lived in Baldwin Home and he owned a Chevrolet truck. (Kenso died in 1999 at the age of 86 or 87. His last rusting truck, a Ford Model A, famous and beloved throughout the Settlement, still sits outside his last Kalaupapa home.)

Kenso was way too old for school, but some of the rest of us went to Mt. Happy School. I stayed for two years, finishing ninth grade. The grades went through high school, but each year the class was smaller and smaller, in a school that enrolled only about 20 kids. What I remember most was having a Victory Garden for a class in farming. We raised head cabbage, Chinese cabbage, carrot, tomato, string beans—and we could sell the crop. But the "victory" part of the garden flew past us. Who cared about Germany?

The teacher tried mightily to get me to continue in school. Her argument was that I needed to be well educated because someday I might get out of Kalaupapa. I should think about my career future.

"For what?" I asked. "I never going get out. No need school for drive one rubbish truck at Kalaupapa."

I was better at going to church than to school. Almost right away I started attending St. Francis Catholic Church. Within three weeks I joined the choir as a tenor, moving into the baritone and bass sections as my voice matured. I had sung at Kalihi, but not Mass. Here we sang the Mass. At Christmas St. Francis was where I first heard—and sang in the choir—"O Holy Night." I tried to be a good Catholic, but I think I failed more than I succeeded.

Over the next five or six years I would hear "Father Damien" over and over. Finally I saw a book called *Damien*. I still remember its red cover.

Until then I didn't know anything. I didn't even know I was in a leper Settlement. Even at Kalihi Hospital, because I was "clean," I didn't believe the stories. I thought I would be immune. Immune, hell. When I read that book, it hit me like a bucket in the face. I read that Damien got leprosy. I would look like the people I saw, with the sores on their faces. Oh! No wonder my parents no tell me. No wonder my father had such a fit at Kalihi Hospital. Just think. I had to read about Father Damien to find out where I was.

The more I read, the more interested I became. I was astounded that he would sail halfway around the world, around South America, to take his brother's place as a priest when he wasn't even ordained yet. I knew I wouldn't do it. I couldn't quite understand why he had come here to care for patients nobody else would, but I knew it was good. Damien made me think about a lot of things, religious and otherwise. He was not one to accept accolades, and I thought about humility.

I had thought that a priest says Mass, teaches catechism, talks religion and tries to convince you that going to church and receiving Communion is the right thing. It was amazing to discover that Damien didn't seem to be about the Rosary and the Mass, but about helping people who were sick and dying. He had a lot of setbacks, with both the Church and the Kingdom's health department not supporting his efforts very well. Somebody else, like me, for instance, would have said, "To hell with it." But he stayed.

I read so much about him that sometimes I felt like I knew him. Of course he was dead and I couldn't see him, but there he was. He became a hero to me, as real as the Boston Red Sox. I actually became a better Catholic. Not a saint, but a somewhat better Catholic. I was still so young that I really couldn't yet apply a lot of the principles to my own behavior. My main reaction was "Wow!" It would be many decades before I attended his beatification in Belgium and experienced the "big wow."

Around this same time, I also learned about my sister Evelyn, stories about her. I heard she had married a man named Winton. I heard that she was pregnant. I heard he was a drunkard. I heard he shoved her. She fell and lost the baby. I heard she died. I believed anything. I did know for sure that neither she nor Christina were at Kalaupapa when I arrived.

Many years later I found out more. Evelyn was 16 when she arrived at Kalihi Hospital in 1927. Two years later she was transferred to Kalaupapa. She did marry Winton, in 1932 when she was 21. She died in 1935. I really didn't remember Evelyn, but I certainly remembered Christina. She came to Kalaupapa in January of 1933. My dear sister who had been so much fun at home in Ninole died in 1935 too, a month before Evelyn. She was only 11.

But when I first came to Kalaupapa, all I knew was that they had been there, and they were both dead.

One day when I was in the store, another patient nudged me and pointed. "See that guy over there?"

I looked.

"He's your brother-in-law."

I stared. "Fuck him," I said.

All of us worked at various jobs—field hand, kitchen worker, janitor, dishwasher, cook, even dressing nurse. We worked six hours a day Monday through Friday and four hours on Saturdays. It came to 26 days a month (except during the summer, when we didn't work) earning a dollar a day. If we were lucky, the Catholic Brother who paid us cash at the end of the month gave us a dollar for every day, $30 or $31.

Then we treated each other at Kalaupapa's stores, Mahelona, Tomita and Kamahana. Sodas, candy, crackseed, pine nuts, root beer ice cream floats in a tall glass. We gambled too, in the pool hall near the Baldwin dining room, dice, blackjack, poker. It was the perfect place. Baldwin Home was situated so we could easily see the cops coming if they decided to try a raid. And the Brothers ignored the gambling. They said, "It's your money. If you want to waste it, go ahead."

They tried to tell us to save it for a rainy day. Brother Materne acted as a savings bank, and sometimes we put some money away with him. But mostly I didn't believe the rainy day would come.

Well, most of us were broke in three days. Which was my condition on the first Sunday of December. After a good breakfast—my favorite was steak and eggs with rice and coffee—the oldest guy at Baldwin Home, Hayashi, who had a radio, turned it on in the dorm, tuning to his favorite Honolulu station. But instead of hearing music, we found out that the Japanese Imperial Navy had just made an unprovoked sneak attack on Pearl Harbor wreaking havoc and destruction on all Hawaiian military bases but especially to Pearl Harbor Naval Base where battleships were being bombed relentlessly. We all crowded around Hayashi's radio, listening to sirens in the background of the news report. Some of the ships in Pearl Harbor had even sunk. In response, the United States had declared war on Japan. We ran outside and we could see black smoke far away, but we didn't know where Pearl Harbor was. It was hard to believe that this was actually happening.

Martial law was declared in Hawai'i. Rumors started to spread that the enemy had landed on several beaches and no one was safe. Sunday night while listening to the radio some more, my thoughts went home to my family, especially Mama and Dad. I knew my older brothers Joseph and Robert—David had died in an accident—would join the U.S. armed forces because they both were already in the National Guard. I had no way to get in touch with any of them because martial law canceled all calls to anywhere for now.

Life in Hawai'i was changed, but it went on. Rationing became a way of life, affecting food, gasoline, everything that was critical. For us, all food and fuel were rationed. A truck was allowed five gallons of gas for a month. It was hard to get poi, so we went without, going heavy on the rice. It got easier when food and supplies started coming by sampan instead of down the *pali* (cliffs) by mule train. The little stores still had some things for us to buy, but we actually put some of our earnings in Brother Materne's "bank." He said to buy war bonds. I think I bought two, but we all thought there was no guarantee we'd live to see the war end. I surely didn't think I'd live that long.

We really didn't like the blackout. All activities ceased at 9 p.m. and the blackout was total. Car and truck headlights were painted black except for a little hole in the middle. In Baldwin Home all the shades were pulled and only the bathroom light was on. We were young and it didn't matter, but lots of patients were quite handicapped and were groping around in the dark, barely able to see where they were going.

Otherwise, at Kalaupapa the war did not touch us at all. No barbed wire fences, no gun emplacements, no military presence. Ironically, although we were essentially imprisoned at Kalaupapa, we had more freedom and privacy and less war-induced hardship than a lot of Hawai'i residents.

In 1942 the last patients to arrive via boat came to Kalaupapa. A group composed mostly of children and teenagers, they were also the last patients to come until sometime later, after the war ended. Sent to Kalaupapa for their safety in case O'ahu was bombed again, their arrival reduced the population at Kalihi Hospital to only 25 or 30. Next to the receiving station was an American "enemy camp" for incarcerated Japanese, Germans and Italians.

Supplies started coming in via mules down the *pali* trail rather than by sea. Mail and movie reels came by trail, and essential items for the official Board of Health store in Kalaupapa. Twice, six or seven new patients came to Kaunakakai via sampan and then down the trail. David Kupele, Sr. and Moses Pauole were hired to make the *pali* trips three times a week or more with Mr. Kupele's horses and mules. Mr. Kupele's son, David, Jr., was a Kalaupapa patient. The animals came down 1,664 feet of cliff on a trail with 26 switchback turns. At the top of the trail, Mr. Titcomb guarded a gate that was about 16 feet tall and 8 feet wide, to make sure no trespassers sneaked through. He also had charge of all freight that came via Kaunakakai, Moloka'i. Titcomb was at the gate from 6 a.m. to 6 p.m. six days a week. The Territory didn't resume using ocean transport until 1945, when it contracted for a weekly sampan freight run and a barge delivery three times a year. Eventually air cargo service replaced some of the ocean service.

Mr. Kupele, who took care of the *pali* freight in and out of Kalaupapa, was also a cowboy and stockman looking after up to 2,000 head of cattle that were fenced out of the Settlement but otherwise ranged free on the Kalaupapa peninsula. Twice a year came the big roundup, when he hired men from Kalaupapa to help out. They were paid $1.25 a day.

We didn't necessarily know how to ride. You just saddled a horse and jumped on. If you don't saddle right, too bad. Nobody helps you. They just call you stupid. You fall off several times and you become self-taught real quick.

I first tried this in a small roundup in July 1942. You reported to Kupele. He would tell you get a horse, saddle him up, feed him barley before you went. Then you're on your way. No big deal.

We drove the cattle to a corral back of the lighthouse and to a larger one at the eastern part of the peninsula. After separating the bulls, steers and calves, we drove the slimmer ones into Waikolu valley, where they would stay for six months for fattening purposes. The rest we drove to Kalawao to the slaughterhouse. Later, the meat was kept at the ice house.

Sometimes we stayed in the saddle all day, out on the range, trying to keep the cattle together. During the roundups, I especially watched Gene Robins, a cowboy from Moloka'i Ranch and one of the best horsemen in all of Hawai'i. He rode, roped and controlled his horse so well that he and the horse were a perfect working team.

I couldn't ride that well, but I was actually a cowboy, not a guy with a bandana covering a tracheotomy! Although I usually didn't read much, I went so far as to read Zane Grey's Westerns. I rode with the roundup twice a year until 1944, when the Boy Scouts cooked up an adventure, and I gave up the life of a cowboy to go camping.

After a three-day roundup, going back to the Baldwin Home routine was especially dull. The salvation from boredom was fishing.

Every Saturday and Sunday, and sometimes on weekdays, about ten of us Baldwin boys would load up Kenso's Chevy truck and the Dodge that Sandbags (Edwin Weatherwax) had and go to the northern shoreline from the airport to about halfway to Nānāoluahine's Cave. Over the rocks we'd bump with our fishing poles and bait or the can with the kerosene lanterns, and flashlights for night fishing. By day, we skin-dived, looking for squid in shallow and deep waters, using both spear guns and long spears. We had goggles, but no fins. Sometimes I'd get spooked by an eel. The best squid area was at Red Camp, a construction camp out toward the airport. We also fished for *manini, pāpio, kole, uhu, kala, nenue* and other fish.

Night fishing was especially fun. We'd ask to get off work early, and usually the Brother would say okay. We'd pile into the trucks, aiming for the best areas out by the airport, Kamahana's Point, Shinsato's Point, Ernest's beach house, fishing from noon to past midnight. When we got to the fishing grounds, we'd each pick our favorite spot on a rock. We fished for *ulua* while it was light, using squid for bait. *Ulua* were anywhere from 6 to 100 pounds. Sometimes something else would come along and cut the line, usually shark or eel. Sometimes we'd catch whopper *pompano*, 15 to 50 pounds. But usually we caught *ulua*.

As soon as the sun began to set, we mixed our bait for *āholehole*—old, old bread and sardines—and lit the kerosene lanterns, making them into spotlights by blocking one side of the chimney. Then watch the *āholehole*! So long as they bite, stay in your place. If they stop, move. But usually they kept biting. They tended to start biting late, so we often stayed until 11 p.m. or a little later, getting home at about one in the morning. In the middle of the night we cleaned the fish, fried them and ate them.

I respected those who I fished with from Baldwin Home, Kenso, Sandbags, Toofy, Wana and others. Some of them were handicapped, but they all were always careful, and always aware of where they were, day or night. They told me what to expect, not just the first time, but always. Most of all, they respected the sea and the open ocean. You were always watching your back, and how you walked along the ledges. Watching, always watching. Watching for that one wave that could kill you. All of us who lived together at Baldwin Home knew each other well, but these particular few I will remember always.

Sometimes we gathered edible things from the river in Waikolu Valley at the eastern end of the peninsula, beyond Kalawao. We went after *hihiwai*, a limpet, or fresh water *'opae*, a shrimp, or *o'opu*, a tiny lobster-like creature. We gathered mountain apples in season, or fresh ginger blossoms to decorate our dining room. Some moonlight nights we'd sneak out, get some gunnysacks and a horse, and walk up the trail. Topside we'd get into a pineapple field and whack off enough pineapples to fill six gunnysacks, then tie the sacks on the horse. Of course we could have asked for the pineapple, but we thought it was better to steal.

Never once did we get caught. Maybe if we had, we would have settled down.

I gave up the cowboy/fishing routine in favor of camping in 1944. That first year, we chose a spot at Kalawao overlooking the ocean, where we could use an abandoned shack that needed only a few minor repairs. It was good, clean ground and the house would be a good place to cook on the kerosene stove and to eat. Kenso was the adult leader. Eight of us boys camped for two weeks, sleeping in two or three tents, going on hikes, going to the ocean, learning to cook with our new pots and pans. The U.S. Army gave us all the camping equipment and we transported it on the Baldwin Home flatbed truck.

We made excursions during the days into valleys and partway up the mountainsides, where we saw wild goats and pigs. The next year, our stay grew from two weeks to a month, then to two months, and finally, in 1946 and 1947, to the whole summer, from May through July. Over the years, our group of campers increased to 18, and finally to 24 boys.

The second year we moved to another, more spacious location at Kalawao and here the camp stayed. It was called Federal Flats, where a federal research hospital had stood in the very early 1900s. In the remnants of the facility we fashioned a makeshift fireplace, installed a kitchen sink, and added a shower even though the water was extremely cold.

We fished and every afternoon we'd go to the beach, but we'd be back while the sun was still high. It helped with our daily cold showers.

Throughout our activities we were cautioned often to be careful to inspect our feet because most of us had little feeling in our feet and we could injure ourselves and not know it. But of course, being kids, we would look at our feet for a day or two, and then forget all about them.

One day I went hunting—barefoot, of course—in Waikolu Valley, and stepped on a broken guava branch. The bottom of my foot hurt, on the ball of my foot between the big and second toe, but it wasn't an open wound. I walked out of Waikolu barefoot and went back to Baldwin Home and let the foot go. I lost whatever feeling I'd had in it.

The wound started off the size of a pinprick and got worse and worse and worse. I ended up in the hospital with an ulcer where the guava stick had poked me.

Then I bought the wrong shoes, with stiff leather soles. I didn't have the money to buy proper shoes and I didn't know how to order them anyway. Those shoes rubbed a break in the skin, and that was it. I had an ulcer on the bottom of my foot.

I thought to myself, "Oh, this will be all right."

How could I know this would become a lifelong problem?

By the time I'd been at Baldwin Home four years or so, I began to love where I was. It was 1945. I wasn't taking any medication, but my health seemed to be improving year by year. I was healthy and strong, and putting on weight as I grew into manhood. We didn't have "Progress" or any of the other humiliations that had pervaded Kalihi Hospital. It was so much nicer than Kalihi that I never once thought of trying to escape up the trail. I only ever heard of three people who tried it. One ended up in the National Hansen's Disease Hospital in Carville, Louisiana, one came back to Kalaupapa, and I don't know what happened to the third.

We lived with the Sacred Heart Brothers in charge. They really cared for us and were never strict. I still remember Brother Tarcissus, Brother

Materne, Brother Louis, Brother Bernard and Brother McGoogan, an Irishman who spoke with a brogue I couldn't quite understand. It sounded funny to me. Brother Patrick Hughes and Brother Dominic Stone, the only ones who were Hawaiian, came later, in 1944.

Brother Patrick cooked for us, and painted. He taught me to paint in oils, sort of taking up where I had left off with Mr. Leong at Kalihi Hospital. Brother Patrick was Irish-Hawaiian-Japanese. Of course, like Damien, he was Catholic. He was like Damien in another way too—he ignored the rules. He ate with us, swam with us, played cards. When we went fishing, he'd get in Kenso's truck and we'd put a burlap bag over his head so he wouldn't get caught.

The Brothers, with Brother Materne in charge, lived comfortably in their own home across from one end of the dorms. They had their own huge dining room and little chapel too.

On Monday and Friday movie nights at Paschoal Hall we had an extra meal. Lots of patients from the other homes or living in individual houses would join us at Baldwin Home after the movies to drink coffee and eat bread, or sometimes leftovers. There was always plenty of food to go around.

The Board of Health contracted with Consolidated Amusement Company for the movies, which arrived with Mr. Kupele coming down the cliff on horseback, and left the same way right after the showing, so the same reels could be used on topside Moloka'i. I remember *The Ten Commandments* and *Quo Vadis*, and bunches of cowboys—Johnny Mack Brown, Hopalong Cassidy, Lash LaRue. We had *The Green Lantern* serial every Friday. At first we had Wednesday movies too, when admission was 25 cents. But soon it was only the free movies Mondays and Fridays. Not even the war interrupted the movies.

About three times a year Baldwin Home would have a party, and we would invite as many guests as could fit in our dining room. Some of us— like when I was a dishwasher—would eat in the kitchen to make more room for the guests.

All the parties were lū'au. The preparations went on for weeks, and it meant a lot of work, but all the able-bodied—about 20 or 30 of the 40 Baldwin Home boys—pitched in. We went to a dry riverbed to pick up porous rocks to use in the *imu*, the underground oven. We dug the hole for the *imu*. We cut firewood, and collected banana stumps to use with the heated *imu* stones to steam the pig and other delicacies. We gathered ti leaves to wrap the food for the *imu*. We caught fish, sea limpets and squid. We got the pig from Johnny Martin. He still lived at Baldwin Home, and he raised hogs for the Settlement.

In the kitchen we, and the Brothers too, prepared chicken with long rice, poi made from taro, rice, and homemade pastries and cakes. We even made ice cream, grinding it in a hand-cranked ice cream freezer, five gallons of chocolate and five gallons of vanilla that we stored in the ice plant until party day.

We prepared the *imu* three days in advance, covering it with a tarpaulin to protect it in case it rained. We butchered and prepared the pig a day ahead. Right before the pig was to be steamed we gathered the banana leaves and ti leaves to add to the oven.

On the day of the lū'au, our dining room would be filled with our invited guests at about 11:30 a.m. They came in casual clothes, but sometimes wore lei around their necks or flowers in their hair. We served the lū'au food on our regular dishes, and beer to go with it. Our entertainment was Hawaiian music. Much of it was instrumental, because we knew the melodies but not the words. I played with the Baldwin Home Boys on the 'ukulele my mother had sent me in the mail—until a *pākē* (Chinese) kid named Ah Wa accidentally sat on it. After that, I borrowed a bass or a guitar. I had learned just by hanging around, although we did have an orchestra too, and because of it I learned to play the saxophone and clarinet. I tried brass instruments but I just didn't have the lips for it. Everybody enjoyed our lū'au music, including some of the other guys on slack key guitar. Sometimes the guests stayed through until supper time and ate leftovers with us. Sometimes they went home in the afternoon and returned for leftovers later. Those times at Kalaupapa—1941 to 1949—were the glory years.

In those glory years, baseball was THE game. McVeigh and the Outsiders—the "Outsiders" were patients who lived in individual houses not part of one of the Homes—were always the teams to beat. Bay View and Baldwin, usually playing on a combined team, were considered mediocre, with not much chance as champions of the league. In fact, we never won the championship.

The umpire was a non-patient named Arnold Smith who worked at Kalaupapa. Of course we all got mad whenever he made bad calls. We played baseball for several weeks three times a year, spring, fall and winter, playing each other team four or five times. We also played volleyball each season, following baseball. This continued despite the war.

Then, one day in August 1945 the war ended. That night we turned the lights on all over the Settlement. No more blackout! No more food or gas rations!

We were in for another change. In late 1945 a small airline named Andrews Flying Service began its new flights to Kalaupapa, offering patients free round trips to the islands of their choice anywhere in Hawai'i. Even though you would have to go and come back the same day, this was a great treat for most patients, and a first! It was a great chance for them to go visit with their families.

The plane carried six passengers, so five of my friends and I flew to the Big Island.

"All us from Hilo," we said.

As soon as the plane landed, I saw my family. We visited until the plane had refueled, then took off again. It was a slow ride back in those days. Ho! It took hours.

The next April was another memorable time, in fact, a cruel time.

On April Fool's Day 1946, my roommate Nicky Ramos woke me up at 6:35 a.m.

"Eh!" he said, looking out the window. "Somet'ing wrong with da water."

"What?" I jumped out of bed and looked out the window. Oil barrels were floating out on the current swinging under the cliffs with the crescent shape of the bay. Pretty soon a whole beach house floated by. Then we heard the radio warning: Tidal Wave Alert! The first of three waves was already coming in, big and fast and wild. I had seen a tsunami when I was small, but where we lived at Ninole we were high above the ocean, and back from it. It had seemed far away. This one we could see clearly.

"Ho!" I said.

"Eh!" Nicky said. "No can see da pier."

Nicky and I went to the dining room.

"You like eat breakfast?" Nicky said.

"Nah," I said. "I like go see tidal wave."

William Wana, Robert Kīhei, Father Peter and I walked toward the *pali* trail and stood watching on the rocks 20 or 30 feet above the black sand beach of 'Awahua Bay. When the water from the second wave came through the lantana bushes in front of us about ten yards, we ran. The waves must have been 35 or 40 feet high. Huge! The water went a mile up the Waihanau stream near Baldwin Home, making the stream so high it almost touched the underside of the bridge.

We came home to Baldwin too excited to eat breakfast, so we jumped on a truck to watch the wave go out by the pier. The third wave washed up over Papaloa Graveyard and flooded the road to the airport. We drove back home and waited for the all clear.

As soon as it sounded, we went back on the truck. The water had torn up the foundation of the wharf, going as high as the steps to the nearby store. It spun the administration office around, but it didn't touch the ice house opposite. It flooded the laundry. It smashed the warehouse door and broke all the windows. Everything stored on the first floor floated right out into the ocean—dry goods, crates, bags of flour and rice—all going with the current toward the lighthouse.

Along the west shoreline, with the current running north toward the lighthouse, the waves had wrecked Red Camp, where construction workers stayed, and all the beach houses. One of them looked like a jumble of toothpicks near where the Lions Club Pavilion is now. It's where my sister

Evelyn used to live.

Papaloa Graveyard's wooden crosses—marking those who had been buried since 1941—were all gone. Heavy headstones from earlier years were knocked over or strewn across the road. Sometime earlier a guy who worked at the cemetery had told me he knew where my sisters' graves were, but I didn't go see them. I thought, "Aah, I go later. Always going be there." Now they were under water. The road by the graveyard was under water too, and so was the airport's grass runway. Later, when the water receded, it left stones all over the grass on the runway. The other direction, the salt water lake stretched to the yards at McVeigh Home. It was five feet deep at the fence line, and that night we came back with our nets. We fished in that field for three days, wading in with a surround net. The water was too deep for that small buggah Kenso, so he stayed on the truck. We learned about the destruction suffered by the other islands, including some people drowning at Laupahoehoe on the Big Island. Our problems were small in comparison, but we had to deal with them. The tidal wave had destroyed the water supply system. What fresh water was available was rationed, and we filled barrels with salt water to flush toilets. A couple of days later, the administration asked the Boy Scouts to help carry pipe to put in a temporary two-inch water line.

Because of the water shortage some people were asked to volunteer to go to Honolulu for a month or two or three. We went by sampan, in groups of six or seven. I signed up and went with the third group. Our sampan left Kalaupapa in the early hours of the morning and arrived at our destination by noon. About seven of us spent three months at Kalihi Hospital. It meant we wouldn't be camping at Kalawao, but we enjoyed the change of being back in Honolulu after being in Kalaupapa for years.

Kalihi Hospital had new faces and we became friends with all we met, patients, staff, adminstrators. I was 20 now, and remembered well the escape routes. The rules and regulations were still in effect but we ignored them. In fact, it was fun breaking them, going through or under the fence almost whenever we wanted. We took up our old ways, movies and pastries.

Asagi Store was still functioning, but the Rex Rooms were gone.

We went under the fence more often than not. It drove the watchman nuts. He knew there was only one possible punishment—send us back to Kalaupapa. And he knew that was no threat at all. He trained his poi dog, Red, to sniff us out. But we fed Red pastries and he became our friend. When we returned from an outing, we'd whistle softly and Red would come, eat a couple of doughnuts, and walk on home to the watchman, who would be waiting on the porch on one side of the building while we went around the other side. Red never even barked.

By September the water supply system was repaired permanently and we returned to Kalaupapa. I couldn't know then that before long I would leave Kalaupapa again. But it would be as a free man.

Freedom

CHAPTER 4

Honolulu 1949

In 1946, after the tidal wave, our lives took a turn for the better because of sulfone, "The Miracle Drug." It had been tested and used on patients at the U.S. Public Health Service Hansen's Disease Hospital in Carville, Louisiana. Every patient using it, whether orally or by injection, took an unbelievable turn for the better, both physically and mentally. Ulcers began to heal after years. Even patients with the most advanced Hansen's disease improved vastly. Three-fourths of the patients improved so much it was hard to believe.

In 1946 results for the first group of patients to use the sulfone drug in Hawai'i came after a short six months. The physical changes were noticeable just as they had been at Carville. Ulcers healed, nodules disappeared, and people took on a different air about themselves. They took more pride in their appearance, which made quite a change, especially among the women. Men too dressed up, especially in white, at the time the most fashionable color for clothing. Until now white had been impossible, with bandaged ulcers likely to stain clothes. Now there was room to compliment someone on his appearance!

We all wondered if it was for real. Was there actually hope for the future now? Was it possible there might be no setback?

I saw patients out much more, allowing themselves to be seen. Some were even thinking of the possibility of "parole," of being released to travel, to go out into freedom. Until now, we had all been under a life sentence that would have to be served in full.

I'd been lucky. I was strong as an ox, and healthy. In mid-1946 I asked for sulfone, electing for the pills rather than the shots. I would take one pill three times a week for two weeks, then lay off for a week. Then back to the regimen.

In the summer of 1947 I had a reaction. I had nerve problems in both arms, a little in my legs, and Bell's palsy. I landed in Kalaupapa's hospital, where the doctor took me off sulfone. It wasn't as bad as the other two reactions I'd had, and within two or three months the palsy and nerve problems went away and I began sulfone again.

Everyone on sulfone went through continuous testing called "snips." Once a month a nurse nicked your skin with a razor blade, to get a skin sample for examination. The "snip" made you bleed. Your snips had to come up clear of disease a certain number of times in a row before you could be considered for "T.R." or temporary release.

Even though the medicine was working wonders, release was not in my mind in the slightest. I was back camping with the Boy Scouts, having my usual summer good time.

But in January of 1949 I left Kalaupapa on T.R. This time it wasn't just a plane ride to Hilo and right back. This time I was flown to Honolulu and taken to Kalihi Hospital. From there I called my mother on the Big Island and told her to come to Honolulu to pick me up. She wouldn't believe me. But finally she agreed to fly to Honolulu—no more boats in this modern time. Later she told me she was skeptical. She thought, "Is he really coming out? Well, there's one way to find out—go to Honolulu."

My father had wanted to come with her, but he had to work. So she came alone. On January 9 I freely walked out the gate I had come in so many years ago and met her.

She had that doubtful look on her face, like "Who do you think you're kidding?" I hugged her and she began to cry.

I held her. "It's all right, Mama. I didn't do anything wrong." I showed her my paper saying I could travel. My cousin drove us to my aunty's house.

When we got there, my mother asked, "Did you run away?"

"No. I told you, I can come out."

"You sure?"

"Yes."

"You not sick?"

"Yes, but not like when I first went in."

Finally she accepted my release. We stayed with our relatives for three days before flying home to Hawai'i. My dad met us at the airport in Hilo and he hugged me. We waited for our bags, then headed for the parking lot. He had a "new" car—a '39 Plymouth.

First we visited Aunty Rachel at Keaukaha. Then we ate out. My parents decided on chop suey. When we finished, we took the leftovers home in little boxes. I didn't even know you could do that.

Hilo had a new look—more restaurants, more night clubs, and a new hotel, the Naniloa. We headed for Ninole. Things had changed along the way. We no longer spent an hour and a half on 21 miles of road winding through tiny towns that hugged the Hāmākua Coast. We were on a straight highway, zipping over long, tall bridges, bypassing all the little towns. We were home in 20 minutes.

The island had taken on a new look, but our house was still the same, though, of course, neither of my brothers was there. During the month I stayed at home, one of the biggest plantation strikes in history was underway, and my father, although he was a *luna*, was helping workers who needed food. Mama was still a housewife.

I loved being home. I even went hunting for Mouflon sheep in the snow of Mauna Kea. But then it was time to return to what had become my life. Mr. Judd, the Kalaupapa adminstrator, sent me back to Honolulu to a rehabilitation school on Dillingham Boulevard. For awhile I lived at Kalihi Hospital and went to the school, where I was put in a mechanics class. We fooled around with cars and lawn mowers. They thought I wouldn't know anything and gave me a simple test in which I was to select screws and bolts. They threw in a couple of nuts too. I chose the right ones—it was duck soup.

"What do you want to do?" a teacher asked me.

"I don't know."

"What do you know?"

"Not much. Mostly farm work."

Boom! I was back on the bolts again. They had mechanical drawing and welding too. The idea was to train people in a trade so they could be self-sufficient. I could do it all. I could have done it blindfolded. Whatever they threw at me, I did. They weren't teaching and I wasn't learning anything new.

After a couple of weeks they asked me again what I wanted to do.

"Art," I said.

"Oh! You have to go to a different school for that."

So, after two months in Honolulu, I returned to Kalaupapa in time for the last campout in the summer of 1949. It turned kind of sour over the problem of merit badges. The scout leaders from Maui who would test us for the merit badges wanted us to try for badges in what they knew. We wanted to try for badges in areas we had learned about—swimming, horses, animal husbandry. I added astronomy to the list.

But no one from Maui could test us in any of those. They weren't about to give us merit badges without testing us, so there went the merit badge program.

But in another way Kalaupapa had become big time in my absence. John Wayne had been there working on *Big Jim McLane*, a film about communism in which the main characters thought someone at Kalaupapa was a Communist. He was the star, and it was his own film company making the movie. In this post-war time the Cold War was just beginning, and communism was a non-stop topic in Hawai'i and all of the United States.

Many of the scenes were shot at the airport, the hospital and Kalawao. John Wayne was gone by the time I got back to Kalaupapa, but later, in Honolulu, I saw him in person and up close at the Waikīkī Theater. Oh yeah, the movie was great!

I was living back at Baldwin Home. On December 3, Mr. Judd called me into the Administrator's Office about 9 a.m. It was a Thursday.

"Come in," he said. "Have a seat."

I sat down.

"How are you?" he asked. I had talked to him before, so he acted kind of casual.

"I'm fine, sir," I said.

Then he got right to the point. "Are you willing to leave Kalaupapa and go out to work?"

I sat there, not exactly surprised, but wondering if he really thought I was a good candidate. He waited for my reply. After awhile I said, "Sure, even today if I have to."

I surprised myself with my answer, but he seemed even more surprised. I think he expected me to say no.

But then he said, "If you want, you can leave tomorrow and be on the job on Monday."

"Yes, sir," I said.

"Leave tomorrow?"

"Yes sir."

"Tomorrow noon will be soon enough." He stood up, shook my hand, and I left. I walked slowly back to Baldwin Home, trying to think if I wanted to change my mind. When I reached Baldwin, I didn't say a word to anyone.

I had just turned 24 years old a month before. Now, after eight years at Kalaupapa Settlement, I was going to be a free man at last.

The next day was a Friday. In the morning I was looking for a suitcase.

"Eh," I asked a couple of guys. "I like borrow suitcase."

"For what, ah?"

"Pack my clothes."

"I no get," they said. But they didn't ask where I was planning to go.

I couldn't think where else to find a suitcase, and time seemed to go by very slowly. At lunch time I ate as usual, looking around at the familiar faces and places. I started to feel sad. I went to the pool hall, but I just couldn't shoot pool. I went to my room. I still had no suitcase, so I pulled a sheet off my bed and piled all my few belongings in the middle. One of my roommates, Lorenzo Costales, came in while I was tying the four corners together.

"You going for real?" he asked.

"Yeah, I going," I said.

"Who going take you airport?"

"Mr. Judd."

"Ah, OK."

"Why?"

"Oh, I just like know, " he said, and he left the room.

Mr. Judd drove up in his car at one o'clock. I picked up the lumpy sheet by the knots, feeling kind of edgy. When I walked out, Kenso and all the gang were there to say good-bye and to wish me luck.

"Where's your suitcase?" Mr. Judd said.

"Right here, sir." I pointed to the sheet slung over my shoulder.

"That's all?"

"It's all I own."

Mr. Judd opened the passenger side car door and said, "Let's go."

All the way to the airport I didn't say a word and neither did he. We got out. I hoisted my sheet over my shoulder again.

"You know what to do when you get there? I've got a place for you to stay," Dr. Judd said.

"Where?"

"The YMCA. And you have a job at Hawaiian Electric Company. You have all the phone numbers you need. Don't be afraid. It's going to be all right."

I nodded.

"Are you sure you won't run away?"

"As long I getting pay, I won't run," I said.

I boarded the plane, the only person on the five-passenger Cessna 402. For the last time, I looked at Kalaupapa, and I felt so sad I almost cried. Several Filipinos had left Kalaupapa, and I heard that one of them had bought a place in Pearl City. But that didn't help. I was still all alone, leaving home again. When we took off, I couldn't look back.

Honolulu loomed into view as we approached. The plane touched down and when it came to a stop, I got off. At first I didn't see anyone I knew.

Then someone said, "You need a ride?" It was the driver from Kalihi Hospital, where I was supposed to spend the weekend before moving into the YMCA. He'd come to pick me up. Oh, boy was I glad!

"Where's all your stuff?"

"Right here in this sheet."

He laughed. "OK. Get in and let's go."

He took me to Hale Mohalu in Pearl City, which had replaced the Kalihi Receiving Station. Judd had been able to get a barracks free from the military after the war. It was on 11 acres, and had been remodeled with both hospital rooms and residence rooms for Hansen's disease patients. Like Kalihi Hospital, it was fenced and guarded, but in some ways it was better, because there was more for patients to do—and it did not have the hated Observation Unit where the doctors put us through "Progress."

I had the option to stay there in a residence room. It seemed familiar, and I didn't know a thing about the Y where Mr. Judd wanted me to stay. It didn't take me a minute to change my mind and stay.

It was almost supper time when I arrived, so I walked down to the dining room. I knew just about everybody, either from Kalaupapa or Kalihi Hospital, so after dinner I hung out there and talked story with them till about nine o'clock. Then it was off to bed in my small but private room.

Hale Mohalu was, of course, much smaller and more confining than Kalaupapa but not nearly so much as Kalihi Hospital had been. The next morning, Saturday, I took the bus to town to get my physical with Dr. Arnold. Mr. Judd had made my appointment. I'd seen Dr. Arnold at Kalihi years ago, when I was a patient and he had been invited to "Progress." Fortunately, this exam, although thorough, was entirely private. He examined me head to toe, nose, throat, tongue, chest, fingers, toes, everything. I was facing a doctor—again. None of us liked it. I know I don't. But what is worse? Knowing you're sick or well? Or not knowing?

Dr. Arnold finally finished and told me I was OK.

After that, I walked around town, went to a movie, and then back to Hale Mohalu. Sunday I jumped on the bus—no need to look for the watchman or go under the fence! I went to Waikīkī, walking around playing tourist. At dark, I went back to Hale Mohalu.

Monday morning I was up early, eager and anxious about what my first day at the Hawaiian Electric Company was going to be like. Mr. Judd had arranged for me to have a job, but I didn't know anything more than to report to where the company was building a power plant at Waiau. I had breakfast, got my lunch, and walked out Hale Mohalu's main gate and down the road a mile or so to Hawaiian Electric. I went through the company gate, checked with the security guard, and asked about the construction site.

I waited with two other new employees, a guy from Hilo named Mahi and a Japanese guy. The reality hit me that I would be working with people I didn't know. It was scary. I wanted to sit down in the corner and cry. But I said I was from Ninole, not mentioning Kalaupapa. Our boss was a Japanese guy from Honolulu and the foreman was a haole called "Tennessee." He must have had a real name, but he was from Tennessee and he spoke strangely. For the second time in my life, I heard the sound of another kind of accent. Tennessee's drawl wasn't a bit like the Irish brogue.

Our assignment was to uncrate boxes of big and small parts and set them up so that other workers could come and pick up the parts they needed. There were valves of all sizes, bolts and nuts, pipes of all sizes and lengths. We did this all day, breaking for lunch together. By Wednesday the job had become routine. But that day held a surprise for me.

Tennessee said, "Henry, they want you at the other yard. Just ask for Mr. Ah Nee. He'll be the guy on the crane."

When Ah Nee saw me, he stopped his machine, jumped down, and we shook hands.

He said, "Go down the warehouse and bring the truck up here. We have to separate that stuff today 'cause they need it in the new plant."

I had never driven any type of vehicle before in my life, let alone a two-and-a-half ton truck, but this is what he wanted. So instead of telling him the awful truth, I went to the warehouse and opened the door. When I saw the flatbed's size, I was in complete shock. Besides that, it was parked so it had only about 15 inches of clearance on each side. I could barely squeeze in the space to get in the cab.

I said to myself, "I'll never get this damn thing out. Number one, I've never touched anything this big. Number two, I don't even know how to drive a car. What will I do with this? But, this is what he wants and he's gonna get it!"

I didn't care if I had to knock all the boxes and crates around. I jumped into the cab and studied the gearshift. I turned the ignition. The engine started. I tried to figure out what to do next.

The gearshift had all kinds of markings so I thought, "OK, here goes nothing." I knew enough to shove in the clutch. I shifted gears and let up on the clutch, and the huge machine started moving backward. At least I was going the right direction. Soon I was out of the warehouse. I couldn't believe I hadn't hit anything or at least done some damage. Right then I could feel myself gaining confidence. This wasn't so hard! Soon I had the truck in the yard and pulled up to where Ah Nee was standing.

"Now go get the finger lift," he said. Another surprise! I didn't even know what a finger lift was. I went to the machine shop.

"Eh! Where the finger lift?"

"Inside the warehouse." A guy pointed.

Of course I'd never seen one, but I was lucky—there was only one vehicle in the warehouse. After studying how it worked, I brought it to the yard. And so began my very first lesson in driving equipment. I worked with the truck and the finger lift all that day and was very happy. What a day!

Thursday was routine until an hour before lunch. Tennessee decided he needed ice for our lunch. Guess who he sent for it? I was to go to Pearl City, about a mile and a half away, pick up the ice, sign for it, and give the man a scrip.

Another new vehicle—a pickup truck! I got the shakes, but I got in and figured out how to work the gears and off I went on the main highway, driving without a license but like I had been doing this all my life! I made it to the store and picked up the ice without smashing into anyone or anything. Friday he sent me again, and the whole of the following week.

I never got a driver's license until 1952.

For eight months I lived at Hale Mohalu, but it wasn't really intended for indefinite residence. Some of the patients were envious and even jealous that I didn't get kicked out. It didn't help that the cafeteria made me sandwiches to take to work for lunch. The jealous ones said I could do anything I wanted because I was Mr. Judd's pet.

I was supposed to become self-sufficient, learning things like how to pay rent. I didn't do any of it. I was just lucky that Mr. Judd didn't come down on my case. Maybe I got away with this because I was the first one to be in this situation. Eventually, though, I had to leave Hale Mohalu. My brother Joseph and I stayed a few places briefly, including the Y. In August 1950 we finally found a studio apartment in Kalihi. He paid the rent and bought food. I got a 25 percent discount on electricity so I paid that and the phone bill.

I continued working at the Waiau generating plant, although now it was nearly finished and I was working inside. We were putting a new generator into place in the plant. All the materials we had set up in the yard we now placed inside. All the nuts and bolts were being put into superheaters, boilers, condensers, layers of pipes, safety valves and more. Everything began to fit, from the first to the seventh floor. But the job was coming to an end, and little by little the company laid off the crew. Finally, it was down to just me and a few others.

One day Tennessee called us into the foreman's shack. "One more week and we have to let you go too," he said. "That will be Wednesday. We'll pay you through Friday."

When the next Wednesday came, we just shut the shop down at four o'clock, shook hands, and went home. Tennessee had been a good boss. I wish I'd known his name.

Without a job I loafed around, spending whole days at Waikīkī on the beach and swimming. I met some of the beach boys, but they were too busy teaching people to surf and taking them out in canoes. Sometimes I went to the movies at the Waikīkī or Kūhiō theaters in Waikīkī, or the Hawai'i or the Princess downtown. I went to so many movies I don't remember them. In February I filed for unemployment, which would be good for a month.

And then I was called to report to Frank Gomes at the Honolulu Power Plant down at Pier 7. Mr. Judd had talked to the company's front office.

Now I had to catch the bus to work. I had long since got over being scared to ride the bus because I thought people would somehow know where I came from and would stare at me. Nobody paid any attention to me. I went to Pier 7, walked into the power plant, and asked for Mr. Gomes. He told me to follow another person named Billy Gomes who was a plasterer. I started working with him. He was good to me, and I learned to plaster walls and pipe, and to do maintenance with the boiler crew. The company hired six other men at the same time, and together we learned everything about how a power plant worked. The company had four power plants downtown and the new one in Waiau. Each of them had to be cleaned annually, a job that took three to six months. We learned from the old-timers all about what makes a power plant operate. We learned how to take it all down and put it back together, from the generators to the boiler room. We worked on one plant after another as a boiler maintenance team. Or at least that's how I felt about working with these guys.

One night in our apartment Joseph and I were eating our supper.

"How you like your job?" he asked.

I told him about the boiler work, and the team.

"How come you no go out?"

It was true, I didn't. All I did was go alone to the beach or the movies. "I don't know." I said. "I stay scared."

"Well, what you going do? Stare at the four walls? You might as well go back Kalaupapa." He ate some more. "Get out. Go to a club or something."

"Why?"

"You not doing nothing with yourself, that's why. What the hell's the sense you stay here, you no going change the way you live?" he said. "Go look for one girlfriend."

"Nah," I said. "I might stay out all night and no can go work."

But in a few weeks something did change. One of the guys on the boiler crew, Roy Freitas, asked me the same questions my brother did.

"What you do when you not working at the plant?"

"Nothing."

"You like join me at the Y?"

I said, "What's the Y?"

"The Y.M.C.A." he said. "Young Men's Christian Association." He told me how he went there and lifted weights.

"It's OK if I join this club?"

"Sure," he said. "Up to you."

And so it began. I didn't know it then, but the Nuʻuanu Y was to be my world and my home away from home.

Now, instead of going home and doing nothing, I could go to the Y. Roy showed me around. I learned to use the gym, the weight room, and the pool. I joined pick up games of basketball and volleyball. Professional wrestlers were working out and they needed someone to spar with, so I learned to wrestle. I could rough and tumble with the best.

I tried a little judo and some Aikido, but they were too strenuous. And boxing—you need good eyes or you can't see the punch coming. I was still as nearsighted as ever, and I couldn't take a chance on boxing. But I was really starting to like weight lifting. I was going to the Y three times a week and really liking not staying home anymore. It felt good.

It got so every time I went I'd meet somebody new—lawyers, doctors, cops, boxers, engineers, musicians, all kinds of guys. I was really enjoying my new life, at work, after work and on weekends. One day I watched the rehearsal for the "Mr. Nuʻuanu Y Bodybuilding Contest." About 15 guys were in it, Japanese, Chinese, Korean, haole, Hawaiian, and they all looked good. They came from all different gyms and they joined the Y to be in the contest.

I set a goal to be a body builder. I worked on it seriously. The joy of meeting weight lifters and professional wrestlers just made it all the better. I never entered the contest, but I stayed with my program for three and a half years. I'd started kind of chubby. Pretty soon the fat turned to muscle. I had a better physique. And a much better life.

At home Joseph said, "You going some place every day."

"I went join the Y."

"Good for you!" he said. "Good for you."

From then on it seemed that only good things could come about. At work the boiler gang became almost family on the job. I felt like the three musketeers I'd seen in movies—"One for all and all for one." There would be slight squabbles every now and then but nothing great. Most of the guys were married, and once in awhile one would need help moving house or furniture. Otherwise, I never went to their homes, but I did meet some of their families. One other guy was single, Aaron, a Hawaiian guy my same age. On weekends we'd go to the beach together, and to movies. Sometimes we'd go to the Moana Hotel and listen to the Moana Serenaders play for the *Hawaii Calls* radio program broadcast from under the banyan tree in the courtyard facing the beach. I even knew one of the musicians—David Kupele from Kalaupapa, the man whose father had brought our wartime supplies down the *pali* trail and who had been the boss of our cattle roundups. He played guitar and bass and he sang. And he was a good composer. After the show, Aaron and I would go someplace to eat. Sometimes we'd go to the new Biltmore Hotel or the Princess Kaʻiulani Hotel, but often, when the band would come back to the Moana in the evening to play for the dance, we'd come too. We never danced, but we'd stay and listen to the music until midnight.

I'd never gone anywhere beyond Pearl City on the one side of Honolulu or Waikīkī on the other. Now sometimes I went traveling around Oʻahu on the bus just to see what there was to see. I'd just ride, jump on, jump off, look for a crowd outside a restaurant—must be good! I could ride for 10 cents, or on the country bus for 50 cents. I went all the way past the airport to ʻEwa Beach on the Waianae side, and out to ʻAina Haina and Kuliʻouʻou on the other end of the island.

After work I would head for the Y gym three times a week. It really felt great to have a place to go to exercise, and soon it became a daily ritual. I lifted weights, played a little basketball, swam a few laps in the pool, had a shower and then went for supper, usually at a Japanese restaurant a block away. By then it would be about 7:30 in the evening and I would go back to the apartment.

I finally felt really free to do whatever I wanted and go wherever I pleased. Nobody could tell me anymore what I could or couldn't do. I finally realized that leaving Kalaupapa wasn't a mistake, but the right choice. I'd been gone almost two years and was loving every bit of it, really savoring this choice I made to move from Kalaupapa and start life anew.

I finally got my driver's license. Joseph took me to the old police station on the corner of Merchant and Bethel Streets. I got only one wrong on the written test. Then a Hawaiian sergeant took me on the road, around the block onto Nuʻuanu Avenue and a few blocks of Beretania Street. I shifted smoothly turning the corners.

"You drive before?" the sergeant asked.

"Nope." Of course it was a bull lie.

"You drive like you've been driving long time. I think you pass."

He cut the test so short that when we got back to the station, the officer there was still doing the paperwork.

During this time our mother died. Joseph, my other brother Robert, and I went to Hilo for her funeral. About a year later, 1952, my father married my mother's sister Rachel. I just couldn't accept this new turn of events. How could my aunty become my mother? But by the time I went home to the Big

Island again in a year or two, it seemed easy. Why be stuck up about it?

At the Y I branched out from the gym and started playing upright bass and singing with the Nuʻuanu Y Serenaders. Enos, on ʻukulele, was retired. Lead guitar man Martin was a fireman and Harry on rhythm guitar was a civilian worker at Pearl Harbor. For quite awhile we performed almost every weekend at different places for various functions—Aloha Week programs, lūʻau, weddings, banquets, even at Hale Mohalu. Sometimes we even got paid. But what I savored most was meeting people from different ways of life.

I even met some of the "greats" in Hawaiian music, including Sonny Chillingsworth and Gabby Pahinui, Myrtle K, Billy Hew Len, the steel guitarist, John K. Almeida, Jackie Flores.

I was at one lūʻau party because I knew somebody who knew somebody who knew we played music. It happened that Sonny and Gabby dropped in too. Someone introduced me.

"You play?" one of them said.

"Yeah," I said. "I do."

I got my ʻukulele—and borrowed a bass—and played and sang with them, real *kani ka pila* style, real impromptu. Those guys were the greatest musicians in Hawaiʻi. Sonny drank wine, and the more he drank, the better he played. Gabby drank anything. And when they both drank, they could play forever.

As for me, I had taken the lifetime cure right after I drank my father's homebrew when I was six.

By late 1952 the boiler gang was working overhauling the entire boiler system and we were working ten hours a day seven days a week. I had to cut back on my time playing music and going to the Y, but even with all the overtime, I still enjoyed the work and the camaraderie.

But the long hours proved disastrous for my health. One day, after a 12 hour shift, we took our usual shower after work.

"Eh, Henry," my friend Sato said. "Get one red spot on your shoulder."

"Ah, nothing," I said.

But when I looked in the mirror, I knew that red spot was a tip-off. Deep down inside I knew I was again reacting to Hansen's disease. I dreaded seeing a doctor, but I knew I would have to sooner or later. I began to watch my body carefully. Within two weeks, more red spots showed up on my chest. Worse, I felt like my strength was leaving me. I knew from before that a reaction tends to do this. I knew I had to go to the doctor.

Monthly checkups would have meant that I would miss a day's work. The Department of Health had instead accepted my promise that I would go to the doctor if something went wrong. I went to St. Francis Hospital, where there was a small Hansen's disease clinic on Mondays. I knew how to get there. I waited my turn, thinking of what this might mean.

The clinic had two doctors. I saw Dr. Chung-Hoon, the doctor I'd seen so many years ago when my mother first brought me to Honolulu. He recognized me, although he couldn't remember my name. He was surprised to see me again.

He looked older. I remembered that he had come to "Progress" at Kalihi Hospital. I was glad to know that the hospital had gotten rid of that crap. He also knew I had been paroled and was working in Honolulu. "What brings you to my office?" he asked.

"I think I'm reacting to the disease." Some time earlier I had stopped taking my medicine because the Department of Health wouldn't give me Diasone, the medicine I had been taking at Kalaupapa.

"How?"

I took off my shirt. He looked at the spots on my chest. Except for them, I seemed to be fine. I was 5-feet-11 and 195 pounds, in good general health. "Well nourished," the doctor said.

"Are you taking your medicine?"

"No."

"Why not?"

"I would have to take one whole day off work just to pick it up. So I never."

"If you had taken it, it would have made a difference. But as it is, I'm sorry, but you'll have to return to Hale Mohalu. The Hansen's disease has reactivated."

"Can I have until Thursday? I'm working at Hawaiian Electric, and I'll have to tell my personnel manager where I'm going and why."

"Sure," he said.

When I had left Kalaupapa, I had several months' supply of pills. To refill the prescription required that I go to the Hansen's disease clinic. Sometimes there were many other patients ahead of me. I never knew how long I would have to wait, so it meant taking a whole day off work at Hawaiian Electric. Worse yet, I didn't want my boss or anyone else to find out why I needed the day off, so I had to make up an excuse. To compound the problem, the clinic would not give me enough pills for longer than a month.

Things seemed not to be going my way in this situation, but the way of the nurses and doctors. I just gave up. I felt well at the time, and for quite awhile longer. But eventually not taking my medication meant the disease came back.

Now I tried not to be stupid. I told myself, "Go get treatment. So what if it takes two years. You can always come out again."

But in two short days my freedom would end! I would have to leave my job, my apartment, my life! I hated the whole idea of being a PATIENT again.

I notified the personnel office and the manager came to see me at the power plant. I told him I would be going to Hale Mohalu the next day, Wednesday. The personnel manager was OK with the situation, and gave me a year's leave.

All of a sudden I was a worried man. It felt like such a loss. I especially worried about whether I would be able to leave Hale Mohalu before the year was up. I wanted to get out in a hurry, but nobody knew when that might be. Not even the doctors could predict it would actually be two years and seven months.

That day in January 1953 I just disappeared. I could not bear to tell the boiler gang. None of them knew where I had come from, and now they wouldn't know where I went. They never found out until more than two years later when I was released from Hale Mohalu and I ran into one of them.

I told Joseph, but he really didn't understand. "I guess it's just one of those things," he said. He decided to stay in the apartment by himself.

The next Saturday the personnel manager came to see me at Hale Mohalu. He was interested in learning about Hansen's disease. He asked to see the lesion on my shoulder.

"Oh!" he said. "I hope you don't mind."

"This is one of the symptoms," I said. I explained more about the disease, how it sometimes reactivates. I explained especially about the sulfone treatment.

"You get yourself well," he said, "And you'll get your job back."

At Hale Mohalu I got sicker, hospitalized flat on my back for three months. It was bad in a different way. When I'd had the reaction at Kalihi Hospital, it was mostly fever. This time it was a rash. I lost weight through stress and worry. Knowing I was seriously sick again took its toll on my mind, and when you worry, nothing goes right. You look at the spots each day, and every day there are more of them and they are worse.

In a few weeks the reaction subsided, and sometime after that I moved from the hospital to Hale Mohalu's living quarters. I got better. And I was a little more mature and gutsy. I'd outgrown pastries and going under the fence was too much trouble, but I walked out through the gate and went to the movies or to a friend's house. I did come back under the fence. To keep busy I did odd jobs around the Hale Mohalu complex—yardman, janitor, painter—as I had at Kalaupapa.

Finally my monthly snips tests stayed clear for a whole year. By the time the doctors decided I was ready to go out again, it was September of 1955.

Joseph came to see me. He'd bought a house in Waimalu and he invited me to live with him again.

So much time had elapsed that my opportunity at Hawaiian Electric had passed, so I had to look for work elsewhere. I got a job with Theo H. Davies Company as a stevedore, but in six or eight months I got laid off.

While I was drawing unemployment compensation I fooled around. For four months I did janitor work in some downtown offices, but I quit.

I didn't call anyone from the old boiler gang, but I got a job at the Y handing out towels in the locker room. Quite a few of them were there, but there was no more camaraderie. I saw it right away.

One of them, a Chinaman from the power plant, knew where I had been. He never said anything, but I could see the fear in his face. I knew the Y was not the place for me. I would make friends somewhere else.

At a party I met a guy named William Lupenui.

"So what you doing?" he asked.

"Not'ing," I said.

"You like job?"

"Yeah."

He got me hired at the Naval Yard submarine base PX, where he worked. I would pump gas and sell beer.

At work he asked me lots of things. When he found out I played music, we started playing together, along with his wife. Pretty soon we were playing for parties. In 1956 I was promoted to the PX warehouse, but William and his wife and I still played music. I was feeling good.

And then, in November 1957, red spots showed up again on different parts of my body. I knew why—once again, I had stopped taking my Diasone, for the same old reason.

I carried a vision in the back of my mind that gave me an artist's view of the disease coming back with a different color and shape, and different feelings. Sometimes I thought it was all an illusion. But of course it wasn't. I could look back and see that each reaction was similar to the others, but also unique. The thing that never changed at all was the fear of the unknown. This ghost kept coming back to haunt me. I went back to Hale Mohalu November 25, 1957. The new reaction was not so bad as before, but after my reaction years ago at Kalaupapa my hands had started to claw a little and the nerves on my left side were affected. I knew there was bound to be more permanent damage now.

But I went on with my life at Hale Mohalu, doing things to keep busy. I played music and participated in a play. I worked in the hospital compound, first as a janitor and yardman and then as a painter.

I even got recruited to be an altar boy in the Catholic chapel. Imagine, altar boy at age 32!

"Nah," I said. "You looking at the wrong angel. I don't know the prayers."

"Ne'mine. If you no can remember the answer, just mumble. Fake 'em."

The first Sunday I mumbled. And I screwed up because I didn't know what to do with the water and the wine. But by the time the second Sunday had passed, I knew the whole Mass.

All this passed the time and provided spending money. We didn't have to go under the fence like we had at Kalihi Hospital. We just walked right out the main gate, caught a bus or a taxi, and went to eat chop suey and see a movie. I remember seeing *From Here to Eternity* and *Samson and Delilah*. But mostly I thought about things. I didn't feel physically in shape to go "outside" again. And with the process of being "snipped" for biopsies it would take another year before the Department of Health would release me anyway.

When I visited Kalaupapa at Christmastime, I took all my belongings, knowing that I was about to make a big decision. I returned to Hale Mohalu briefly, but early in 1958 I told the Department of Health I wanted to go back to Moloka'i.

I was 32 years old. I'd move back, work there, work for my pension. In one way it made some sense. But in another I was in the midst of the agony of defeat. I had given up the idea of ever going outside again.

Down in the Naʻau

CHAPTER 5

Kalaupapa 1958

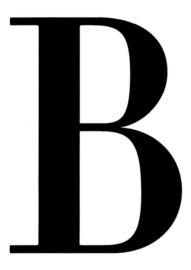

aldwin Home had been dismantled in 1950-51. Many of my old friends were living elsewhere in the Settlement. I moved into the big building of McVeigh Home. All 12 rooms were vacant. Everyone else had moved into the cottages. Within a short time, I moved again, to the large Quonset hut that had been remodeled into living quarters for single men. Kalaupapa had a new Department of Health Administrator, but otherwise nothing much had changed. The patient population was about 375.

My friend Francis Chong was the labor foreman, and he offered me work as a janitor and cleaning yards. And I did drive the rubbish truck, just as I had predicted to the teacher who had tried to make me stay enrolled in school. I took the jobs just to keep busy. In 1959 I became a carpenter. It was another of my many "learn on the job" situations. I just picked up a hammer and started repairing buildings.

I was home. At the Y they had been thinking I was a different person because I'd been having treatment at Hale Mohalu. Here people were my friends no matter what. They were glad to see me.

Toward the end of the year Kalaupapa's sheriff, William Malo, asked if I was interested in an opening in his department. At one minute past midnight on New Year's Day 1960 I became one of Kalaupapa's four policeman. I was 35. I had already worked in the patient employment system 10 years, so by 1970 I would be able to retire after 20 years' service.

The first few months I worked the night shift. We had khaki uniforms. We weren't armed, but had the option of carrying a night stick. None of us did. The stick is only a threat. It's better to talk to people. We dealt with an occasional vehicle accident, but most of our calls were for domestic problems or "disturbing the peace" with loud, late-night parties where there was too much drinking. If we couldn't talk down drunks, we'd put them away for safekeeping in the jail, which had 12 cells for men and 2 for women. Each had a bed with a hard mattress, and bars in the window—no glass or screen. We'd tell the guys to have a friend bring pillows or blankets. In the morning they'd be sober. We never actually arrested them or charged them—then we'd have to go to trial. In my ten years with the department, we only took four or five cases to trial. Most of those few were convicted, and then paid a fine or went to jail. The longest sentence was 15 days.

The only really big case had happened before I ever came to Kalaupapa. Sometime around 1940 the same guy who had told us about the Rex Rooms when I was a kid at Kalihi Hospital had been sent to Kalaupapa. He'd come to Kalihi from prison when he contracted Hansen's disease. When he was committed to Kalaupapa, he somehow smuggled in a .22 rifle. He got in an argument with another patient in the Kalaupapa Hospital, and shot and killed him right in the hospital. Both of them were two damn fools. A few days later, the killer was shipped back to prison in Honolulu, where he later died.

The year I joined the police force, the department reorganized so that each officer and the captain took a six-hour shift each day, and one guy could have a day off. The sheriff was on call all week around the clock.

Crimes anywhere are always found out somehow, even in remote places, and Kalaupapa is no different. But the criminal element is so small in such a place, nothing major happened in all the ten years I was an officer.

During those years, my father died. He was 75, born the year Damien died, in the reign of King Kalākaua. He'd been a little kid at the time of the overthrow of the monarchy in 1893. In April of 1964 I went to Hilo for his funeral, and then returned to Kalaupapa.

Police patrol had become routine. A new staff person broke a little of the sameness, a black guy named Marion Butler, really down to earth, always ready to talk. He did lab work and blood tests. The best thing was that he was fun. But soon I developed another new routine that included a stop at Bayview Home overlooking the ocean.

A young patient worked evenings at Bayview as a steward, helping care for the blind. A few months earlier she had separated from her husband and moved to Bishop Home. I seemed to gravitate toward Bayview when my police shift ended and her work shift began.

She was Chinese-Hawaiian, about 11 years younger than I. She had arrived sometime during the years when I was "outside." She'd come to see me after work, and each time she would stay a little longer. I told myself—a lifetime bachelor who had never had a single thought of marriage or anything even close to it—I should avoid this. But I really didn't try. I was thinking of an old Ink Spots song. The words said things like "If love is to grow there's got to be a glow to you. Each door has a key." That's how I started feeling about falling in love.

I had a '52 Chevy, and I started taking her to work and bringing her home. We'd go riding, then hiking up Kauhakō Crater, or into Waikolu Valley. Often we'd go to her room at Bishop Home where she'd cook something on her two-burner hotplate and we'd watch TV.

It got so we were together everywhere, day and night. We knew we could live together, and it was good.

About a year later, in March 1964, I went to Oʻahu to shop for things we needed, mostly food items we couldn't get at Kalaupapa, especially Chinese and Japanese things. I stayed a few days with friends in Kailua. One evening I was playing canasta with my friends when the phone rang. It was for me. The game stopped while I took the call. It was my sweetheart.

"Eh, Henry," she said. I could tell she was all excited about something. "I just wen' find out I stay *hāpai* (pregnant)."

I was stunned. She had been married to someone else for years and never had a kid. We had never talked about it, but I had assumed she'd been sterilized. "You sure?" I finally said.

"I know I sure!" She sounded so happy.

"Ho!" I said. "We going get married." And I hung up.

The guys all looked at me.

"Wow!" I said. "My wife is pregnant!" Of course she wasn't my wife yet, but it wouldn't take long to change that.

"Eh, brah!" one of the guys said. "You one fadda now!"

"This is the damnedest thing I ever heard!" I said. But I liked it. In fact, I was elated. But it also occurred to me immediately that there was a government rule that no child born to parents with Hansen's disease can be kept or raised at Kalaupapa or Hale Mohalu. For the moment, I put it out of my mind.

We resumed the canasta game but I didn't care anymore if I won or lost after that most important phone call from *my wife*. My sweetheart would be my wife! And we would have a baby! Wow!

I went home in three days, and we hugged and hugged and hugged. We were both happy about the child. Anyway, we made plans to marry. I felt scared of all the rigamarole in church weddings. What if I said "No" when I should say "Yes?" I didn't want any fanfare or parties or fancy stuff. I just wanted a wife and a child.

My sweetheart came to Honolulu and we went out and got a ring. The Hale Mohalu administrator, Mr. Mendonca, asked a judge to do the ceremony. We were married at 5 p.m. in the middle of a week, in Honolulu at Hale Mohalu. Our witnesses were two other patients, our friends Jim Brede and Mary Ishiki. We stood before the judge in the lobby, my bride wearing a muʻumuʻu and I dressed in a blue shirt and black slacks. When it was all over, in just ten minutes, Jim, Mary and the two of us went out for chop suey.

Legally speaking, my wife was an active patient still confined to Kalaupapa and therefore to Hale Mohalu, so in order to go out to the chop suey house in Pearl City she had to go "under the fence." We returned after dark, and spent our honeymoon at Hale Mohalu.

That weekend we returned to Kalaupapa, to McVeigh Home, where those old single rooms had been changed into apartments.

We never figured on having a child—at least I didn't—but here it was, my wife was pregnant. She lived through it like a queen, getting larger and larger. I thought more and more about the rules about babies. The government laid down this law. Even the Patient Council could have nothing to say about it. At Kalaupapa we would not be able to raise our child.

All patient births were through Hale Mohalu, so about two weeks before the baby was due we flew to Honolulu again. Then, on Wednesday, November 2, 1964, my wife was taken to a private room at St. Francis Hospital. Between 11 a.m. and noon she gave birth to a baby girl. We had agreed that if the baby was a boy, she would name him. If a girl, I would choose the name. I had decided on my name weeks before her arrival, the most beautiful name I could think of. I wanted to give her a Hawaiian name too, but one that everyone could say easily. Once, years earlier, I had had to sign a draft card with my full name: Henry Kalalahilimoku Nalaielua-aʻa-kamanu. The draft board guy had said, "What the hell is this?" Since that episode, I have never used the entire thing. So I chose my baby's name carefully. It means a small, heavenly cloud. And that's exactly what she seemed like when a nurse brought me the small warm bundle that was her, my baby. She was a small cloud from heaven. I cuddled her in my arms. She was so tiny and cute. Her eyes were open and she was moving her head, trying to guess what was what. This was my baby, and she looked like a little angel. I was too happy to cry.

But soon I had to face the rest of the situation. Because of Hansen's disease, and because my wife was not a "parolee" like I was, she was separated from everyone else, confined to a private room in strict isolation—isolation even from her own baby. That was the rule.

Here I was, the happiest I had ever been in my life, and my wife was not even treated like a human being. There are no words to describe how much it hurt.

I was permitted to visit my wife in her room.

"Are you happy?" she asked me.

It was hard to answer her. Finally I said, "Yes."

Her reply spoke a lot more than the few words she uttered: "I'm glad for you."

She and I had talked about what we would do next, but had not come to a conclusion. Department of Health rules meant that we could not raise our baby at Kalaupapa. Yet she wanted to keep our little girl. That would mean we would have to live on O'ahu. But how?

"Welfare," my wife said.

I pictured myself as a father. Maybe not the best, but a father nonetheless. I whispered to myself, "I have a daughter!" But I had to face the situation. "No," I said. "No welfare. And you know that if we leave Kalaupapa, it's for good."

My wife persisted.

"It's good to raise a child," I said. "But only in the right environment. Our future is dim. For all of us." I'd seen an aunt go on welfare. I didn't want that for us. And what if the disease flared up and one—or even both—of us had to go to Hale Mohalu?

Right before our baby was born I had talked to my second-oldest brother, Robert, and his wife, Nani, telling them our problem and asking if they would accept our baby and raise her. They had two teenagers, a son and a daughter. They agreed to take the baby.

My wife finally saw that I was making more sense than she was. She still wanted just a glimpse of the baby. The hospital's answer was "No." This time, she cried.

I was there the next day when Robert and Nani came. My little girl was wrapped in a pink receiving blanket. Nani took her from the nurse, rocking her in her arms.

After my wife's mandatory three-day isolation, she and I flew home to Kalaupapa.

I know these things are harder on the mother. But I also know we made the right decision. Yet, I think if it had not been Robert who was taking our baby girl, I would have accepted welfare.

Even though my wife didn't cry or scream, I knew just by her looks that her world stood still. She had just given birth to a beautiful little daughter and she was not even permitted to hold her own baby.

After a year or so, Robert and Nani asked to adopt our daughter, whom they treated as if she were their own child. I thought it through. They had raised her from day one. My wife and I lived at Kalaupapa, where we couldn't have her. She didn't like the idea, but after we met with Robert's attorney in Honolulu, she agreed. Our baby would still be a Nalaielua, but she would grow up as my brother's daughter.

Back at Kalaupapa, I went back to work with the police and my wife took a job as an orderly in the hospital. We moved from the apartment to a more comfortable two-bedroom cottage that had a small yard and a garage area. She got her parole, and we'd go out to Honolulu every once in awhile to shop for things we needed or wanted—furniture, linens, kitchen utensils.

If I was in Honolulu alone, my other brother, Joseph, who was still a bachelor, and I always made it a habit to visit our brother Robert. When my wife and I were together on Oʻahu, sometimes we'd visit. But it was awfully hard on her, so she didn't come very often.

In a way, Robert put restrictions on visiting. He never really said anything, but there was not a warm and embracing feeling. I could tell Robert and Nani had an uncomfortable underlying suspicion that their daughter might get the disease from my wife. I could feel them pulling away. That was the trouble in those days, people just didn't understand about Hansen's disease.

If Joseph had been married, I think he would have taken our little girl. I was close to him, but not to Robert. But Robert was her father now.

We could feel his "law," and all of a sudden we'd have to leave.

I think my wife always wanted to say to our growing daughter, "I'm your mother." The little girl never knew if my wife was her Aunty or what. She knew me as Uncle Henry.

As she grew out of babyhood, it was plain she was full of mischief. I think that came more from me than from her mother. It became too painful for my wife to keep visiting, but I continued until our daughter was about 15. Finally the hurt got to me too, and I stopped visiting. Eventually Robert and Nani explained to her about her birth, but I was still "Uncle Henry." Then, all of a sudden, it seemed, she graduated from high school and was out and working. Later she moved to California. Sometimes now we talk on the phone.

****

I was definitely a married man, not a carefree bachelor anymore. Besides that, in 1968 I was promoted to captain in the Kalaupapa Police. I got a little raise in pay, but now I was on call when the sheriff was absent, and I was always responsible for the officers' actions. If anything went wrong, I was the guy in charge.

The next year the sheriff ripped his leg on coral while he was diving. The infirmary transferred him to St. Francis Hospital in Honolulu, and I was suddenly Acting Sheriff, with responsibility for the whole Settlement— 7 days a week, 24 hours a day. Fortunately, nothing of law enforcement import happened during the four months the sheriff was gone.

He returned a few months before I reached the 20-year retirement time. He said, "Henry, work another year and get my job. Then you retire with a bonus."

"No," I said. "Not on your life." I'd taken the job with the intention of working a total of 20 years in the patient retirement system, and I would leave as soon as I completed the time.

I worked until March 1, 1970—forgetting that I had two weeks' vacation pay coming. But that's the way it was.

A month later the officers honored me with a Chinese dinner at one of the private beach houses at Kalaupapa. Of course we played music all the time, so we provided our own entertainment on this occasion. They gave me a gold plaque and a gold captain's badge. I still have the plaque, but I'm not sure what happened to the badge.

My idea now was to go to Honolulu and get a job there, to supplement the small pension I now received. Joseph's house in Waimalu had three bedrooms, and I knew we could live with him. But my wife and I weren't getting along so well, and she did not want to go to Oʻahu. We finally decided I would go and she would come later.

It was May 1970. I went to Honolulu, and for two weeks I was a live-in babysitter for four teenagers while their parents, friends of mine, went on vacation. I stayed with them in their apartment on Kapiʻolani Boulevard. The three girls were OK, but the boy wouldn't do what he was supposed to. His parents were quite strict, and with me on duty as Papa and Mama, he took advantage and went out whenever he wanted.

I saw an ad in the paper for positions with a new security company, Wackenhut. The sergeant read my resume and hired me.

I was assigned to apartment garages and other private parking lots to monitor illegal parking. My job was to see that the offenders removed their cars. I also worked at a coffee house in Waikīkī, watching for people who ordered a meal, ate, and ran out without paying. Dole Pineapple Cannery became my permanent assignment. It was in Iwilei, the same district where Kalihi Hospital had been, and it brought back memories.

The Dole compound was the biggest place I had ever worked. Over a period of months, I worked every shift and learned to know every corner of that cannery. I was one of about six officers under two sergeants and two lieutenants.

I watched employees steal cases and cases of pineapple, and soda too, which the company also made. My job was just to report it. A Wackenhut lieutenant had to do something about it. In that respect, the job was a lot easier than policing Kalaupapa.

When I started with Wackenhut, I moved in again with Joseph, in his house in Waimalu. Every now and then my wife would come to visit. I bought a second-hand car from a friend who owned a junkyard, Lionel Kekipi, a former patient. I asked him for one that ran pretty well and he made me a deal I couldn't refuse, for $350 cash. So my wife and I went riding, or shopping.

Once we went to celebrate our daughter's birthday at Robert's house and I played and sang with my brothers. Although I had played a lot of music both at Kalaupapa and around Honolulu, I had never played with them before. They were remembering the days of our childhood, when they played but I could only sing. Now they were stunned when I played in all kinds of keys. The look on their faces pretty much conveyed "Hah?" And then they said, "Boy, you're good."

Things with our marriage seemed to be fine, and right before Christmas I flew home to Kalaupapa for a few days. But when I got there, I got the cold shoulder.

"Why you come home?" she wanted to know.

"This is my house," I said. "It's where I belong."

She cooked, and we went riding in the evenings, at my suggestion. But mostly she ignored me. It put me on edge. I wondered if she was up to something. I couldn't pinpoint anything, but something wasn't right. The reception she gave me made me think that when I left again, I'd stay away longer.

I spent New Year's with a family on the Big Island, the future in-laws of a former patient, Oliver Kelly, who had come back to Hilo to be married. He and his fiancée had met when they were students at a Honolulu hair stylist school.

I flew from Hilo back to Honolulu, back to work at Dole. I took a second job, pumping gas during the days at a station on Nimitz Highway, while working at Dole nights. At first it was easy. But then—as it had before—working too much took its toll.

The service station was busy, and it was good money. But in both jobs I was on my feet all the time. After several months, I began to notice my foot acting up. It was the left foot, the same one that had developed an ulcer in the area of the first metatarsus years earlier, in the forties. The problem was compounded by the fact that Hansen's disease damages nerves, and it left the foot without much feeling. It's easy for such a thing to grow from the size of a pin prick to as large as a silver dollar—and get infected too. Unless I looked at the bottom of my foot, I wouldn't know anything was wrong.

Not only that, but all of a sudden I developed another problem common among us patients, "drop foot." On the same foot! You're unaware that anything is wrong and then one day you wake up, and BOOM! You step down fine but the foot won't come up. When you walk, if you aren't watching, you trip on your own toes. But it was a mechanical problem I could live with. I went to see the doctor—for the ulcer.

"Stay off your feet," he said, and gave me some medicine to put on the ulcer.

But it kept getting worse. I knew in my heart that sooner or later I'd have to go back to Kalaupapa. Working two jobs was not worth it. It never was.

***

Early in 1971, I was still in Honolulu, living with Joseph. All of a sudden my wife called on the phone.

"I coming to Honolulu," she said.

When she flew in, I met her. I was shocked when she got off the plane. I could see she was pregnant. She said the obvious: "I stay *hāpai* again."

She was thinking that maybe we would go on welfare and raise this second child. I didn't have to stop and think.

The baby was another girl. I saw her once. A Moloka'i couple adopted her.

I speak of all this as if it were easy. It was not. I kept thinking: Am I doing the right thing? Am I on the right track? Am I doing myself and my wife justice? Am I doing the baby justice?

I relived the whole experience of our first little girl's birth. Once again, a child was born but could not be raised by her parents. This new situation was even more complicated, and, like before, hardest on my wife. Kalaupapa is a very small place, and of course everyone there knew all that was happening.

At the end of 1971, I left and went back to Kalaupapa. It had taken awhile for my wife to really understand the need for the second adoption, but I think she had come to accept it. We were getting along better than we had in a long time.

Back at Kalaupapa I paid more attention to my foot. The ulcer on the bottom was an open sore bigger than a quarter. Sometimes it would get infected, and had to be dressed twice a day, and sometimes putting on my shoe was a problem. It made me limp. And yet I didn't feel a thing. I learned that a Dr. Nemechek had a new method for healing such an ulcer by putting the foot in a cast. I went back to O'ahu to Hale Mohalu to see him.

He explained that the idea was that keeping the foot immobile would allow the ulcer to dry and the surrounding skin to slowly close the wound. I expected that if he cast my foot I would not be able to walk at all, but I was wrong.

"It's a walking cast," he said. "We'll leave it on about six weeks. The ulcer might heal in that time. Or, if it is not completely healed, we can put on another cast."

The next morning Dr. Nemechek put on the cast. It took three days to dry before I could walk on it.

"If you need to walk a lot, get a wheelchair," he said. I went back to Kalaupapa. In six weeks I returned to Hale Mohalu. I'd worn the cast down to an eighth of an inch from walking all over the place.

"You're walking too much," the doctor said.

It was my fault. I'd walked too much and broken the cast. Even so, when he removed the cast, I was amazed. The ulcer had shrunk from two inches to about a half inch wide, and it looked ready to heal.

Dr. Nemechek recast my foot. But it was a mistake to let me walk. After several more casts, the foot still had not healed completely. Dr. Nemechek was giving up.

"I think you should see Dr. Brand," the doctor said. "He's in Carville, in Louisiana."

I had heard of Carville from other patients. It was the location of the national Hansen's disease center near Baton Rouge. Dr. Paul Brand was the ultimate expert at healing foot ulcers by casting.

It was now May 1972. Dr. Nemechek suggested I go to Carville in July or August.

I went back to Kalaupapa and talked it over with my wife. Things were going better for us. As far as I was concerned, the past was gone and we could start over. I really wanted to stay married. Looking back, I think that despite our differences, we lived well together. I was more fortunate in being married to her than she was married to me. She was a very good housewife, and a good, kind-hearted person too. And me? I didn't do much to help her. I was glad she agreed to go to Carville with me.

Two other patients would go too, Timothy Waiamau and Eddie Marks. Eddie had been at Carville before, but he couldn't stand the cold of winter and he came home. Now that it was summer, he was willing to try again.

Other Kalaupapa patients who were still at Carville made a special request.

"Eh! When you guys come, bring Hawaiian food," they said. "We hungry for local food and this place no mo' not'ing li dat."

So in July we fished for *aku*. We gathered *'opihi*. We made *kalua* pig. We put it all in cold storage until our departure, an enormous amount of fish and shellfish, poi, *'opihi*, raw fish, *poke*, *kalua* pig, *lomi* salmon, kim chee, daikon, fishcakes and pineapple. We gathered a whole box of green coconuts. I got so excited I could hardly believe the day of departure had arrived—and it hadn't! It was July 20 and I was still in my own bed, waking from a dream. I had another month to wait.

Finally we packed our suitcases—two each. We'd been told to take warm clothing because it might snow. We thought that meant sweaters, because that was the warmest we had. We stuffed the sweaters in our suitcases. Then all of us piled our suitcases and the six or eight boxes of cold storage food on the baggage cart at the little open-air airport at Kalaupapa. Other patients, nurses and friends came to say good-bye.

In Honolulu, the driver from Hale Mohalu could hardly believe we were taking so much food and clothing. It was true, the pile was enormous, a huge contrast to the small lumpy bundle I brought when I first came to Honolulu in 1949 with all my belongings tied up in a bedsheet.

At Hale Mohalu we got our Braniff Airlines tickets, had lunch, and then an early supper before our flight at 4:05 p.m. Friends gave us each a double carnation lei. At the airport we went through the regular agricultural inspection and then a special customs inspection because of Hansen's disease. Nothing went wrong, and all our precious food passed inspection. We got our seat assignments and boarded the plane. I carried on an overnight bag and my 'ukulele. The plane was a Boeing 747 and it was huge, with rows and rows of seats, 448 to be exact. It would fly at more than 500 miles per hour at an altitude of almost 40,000 feet.

I remembered the first time I ever flew in a plane back in the forties – it had six seats. On this jumbo jet I felt unreal and lost. I was a *kua'aina*, a country jack who had never seen anything that big.

After take off I ordered a rum and Coke. My wife had a Coke. We were fed supper—again.

I'd traveled to all the other islands, but this was my first trip to the mainland. My wife's too. I figured my foot would finally heal. I wondered about the new place we were going, almost 5,000 miles away. What would it be like? Louisiana was supposed to very French. What would that mean? What people would we meet? Would some of them be black? What food would we have? After all, the Hawaiian food might last three days. I settled into my seat for the long trip.

It was August 22, 1972. We expected to stay three months.

Carville

CHAPTER 6

Louisiana 1972

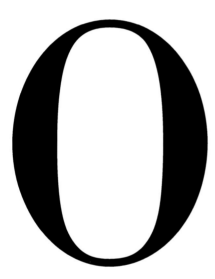

Our overnight flight stopped in Los Angeles but we didn't get off the plane. About 7 a.m. the plane circled New Orleans Moisant Airport several times and then landed in a maze of fog. We were to stay on the plane until we were called.

Finally we heard a voice on the intercom—a Southern accent with a French overlay. We didn't understand a word. At last Eddie caught his name—Marks. "Waiamau" and "Nalaielua" were beyond recognition. "Henry" came out in the French way, Henri—Ahn-REE.

We walked off the plane to meet the Carville driver.

"You're the people with the funny names!"

I looked at his nametag: Whitemore. I looked at him, a big black man. "No, you have the funny name!" I laughed. And he laughed. Whitemore couldn't believe the size of our pile of baggage and boxes, but still, we were off to a good start. We helped Whitemore jam it in the van, and then we got in.

"Relax," he said. "We've got quite a ride."

"How far?" I asked.

"Eighty-five miles."

"My God! That's far enough to go around our Settlement 12 times!" Back home we had 18 miles of paved road, Kalaupapa's perimeter road accounting for 7 of them.

The countryside was a crisscross of country lots and super highways and small towns. We saw several plants we didn't recognize. Finally we came to a fence line.

"Carville's straight ahead," Whitemore said. "Welcome."

The Hansen's Disease Center looked like a prison, like Kalihi Hospital, with a wire fence in the front and a sentry at the gate. We drove through and stopped in front of a big two-story building. Later we would find out that buildings in a huge quadrangle housed everything. We found out that one of the main means of transportation within the compound was bicycles, but also that patients could have their own motor vehicles they could use on passes good for 8 to 72 hours, or even up to a month, with permission.

We would soon find out that Carville was 70 percent black. Of course there were whites, but also Chinese, Japanese, and many from Puerto Rico, Jamaica and the West Indies.

Sylvester Pauelua and Rosalyn Wong Kato, two of the seven patients already there from Kalaupapa, came to say hello. Handshakes, hugs and kisses all around, and then the time of yakking was over. Eddie Marks told us how the National Hansen's Disease Center at Carville was better than Kalaupapa—the hospital had more nurses and doctors, and each patient was assigned a particular doctor.

Mrs. Kanatani, the doctors' secretary, checked us in, took roll, and made us medical appointments for the next morning. She took us men upstairs to the men's hospital ward. Our boxes of food were taken to a refrigerator at the Protestant chapel.

"Hi, y'all," said the day nurse, Lillian Stevens. It sounded funny to us.

"Aloha!" I responded. She greeted us her way and I responded in mine.

Each of us took a cubicle—bed, table, closet, that was it. We took our necessities out and put our suitcases in a closet. Then we changed into hospital pajamas.

Pretty soon Rose and my wife came upstairs. Now we found out there was not enough housing for couples and we would be on a waiting list for an apartment.

Meanwhile, my wife needed to know where she was going to stay. No one had told her. We hadn't known this before, but unless she admitted herself as a patient, she would have to find her own place to live away from the Hansen's Disease Center. She decided to sign in as a patient. All she would need was a room. She got one in House 15-2, which meant it was upstairs. Each floor of this women's house had 12 rooms. She had Room 6 upstairs. Because of my foot, I was to be in the hospital.

We were served an early supper in the hospital, but I wasn't interested. I was thinking of all the Hawaiian food waiting for us at the *pa'ina*, the feast we would have around 7:30 p.m. in the Protestant Chapel.

All the Hawai'i patients came—besides the four of us, it was Rose Kato, Tad Higa, and Sylvester Pauelua, and Nancy and John Deraine. We invited several others, including Grace Choy, Meximo Gonzalez, and the Protestant chaplain Oscar Harris and his wife, Juanita. So it was a good-sized family gathering.

Of course we had to explain all the food to the non-Hawaiians.

"What is this 'po'?" one of them asked, in that soft Southern accent.

I laughed. "Poi," I emphasized the "oy" sound. "Poi."

"Where does it come from?" they wanted to know.

They stumbled on *'opihi*, the little limpet we love to eat raw. They were sure it was "O-pee-HIGH."

"Oh-PEE-hee," we laughed.

"What is it?"

We introduced them to daikon, the Japanese pickled radish.

"Day-con," they said.

"Die-con," we corrected. We all laughed.

They all tried these things they couldn't pronounce, but they liked only the pig and the pineapple. They thought kim chee, our beloved, hotly delicious but odorous Korean pickled cabbage, could start World War II all over again.

After we ate more than our fill, Higa set up his two-decker steel guitar. I opened my ‘ukulele case, and we started playing. We picked songs we hoped everybody knew, "O Makalapua," "Akaka Falls," "Ua Like No A Like."

It turned out that Juanita was a professional pianist and played as the Protestant chapel's organist. We had one of the Charles E. King books of his Hawaiian songs, and she could read the music and play along with us. Meximo Gonzalez, a patient who had been a professor in Puerto Rico, played guitar in spite of having lost all his fingers. He just played with the stumps, and it was fantastic. He was really happy to meet us, fellow musicians, and after that we played together all the time.

About 9:45 p.m. we checked back into the hospital and my wife went to her quarters.

In the morning breakfast was at 7:30 a.m., but everything hums from about 5:45, when janitorial work begins.

After breakfast we met medical staff—doctors, physical and occupational therapists, Sisters of Charity nurses, and the Catholic chaplain, Father Oscar Bergman. We were each assigned a doctor.

It was sort of like my first day at Kalaupapa many years earlier, when I had gone riding around the Settlement. Here I learned about the laboratory, the canteen, and Lake Johansson, a manmade lake named for a well-loved man who had been a doctor at Carville some years earlier. It was dug, filled, and stocked with trout and bass, and then rowboats were provided so patients could fish.

Carville was a maze of walkways. The buildings around the huge quadrangle were completely screened. We soon found out why. The place was buzzing with bugs, including mosquitoes the size of spiders.

There was a laundry room, a reading and TV room, a theater that showed movies once a week, a library, offices for the chaplains, social service workers, and physical and occupational therapists. There was a school, shoe shop, carpentry shop, rooms for a dentist and the doctors, and a records room. There were patient rooms upstairs and downstairs, a bank, and offices for *The Star*, a magazine published by the patients and distributed in 109 countries and the entire United States. Of course the complex included the hospital and operating rooms. There also were cottages for married couples and staff. The dining hall served breakfast at 7:30, lunch at 11:30, and supper at 4:30.

The complex had one nine-hole golf course for patients and another for staff. There was also an armadillo farm that raised the animals for medical experiments. You would think that because of their armor armadillos wouldn't be able to move much, but they are really agile. It was some months before I saw them at the farm. They were about the size of a big puppy, and they didn't make a sound.

The grounds were full of pecan trees, and when they are in season in the fall, everyone picks them up. Just shell them and eat them. I like them better than walnuts.

The doctors were top-ranked specialists. The surgery most talked about was the tendon transplant, done especially with patients who had cerebral palsy, clawed fingers or toes, or drop-foot. Paul Brand, the surgeon recommended to me by Dr. Nemechek, headed the tendon transplant team, which included Dr. Carl Enna. Brand's wife, Margaret, was another fine doctor, an ophthalmologist. Paul Marchand was the podiatrist, and Dave Welch was there to make orthopedic sandals.

The school did not impose any age limit. Most of us Hawaiians attended to learn to speak Spanish so we could talk to the many Mexicans and Puerto Rican people at Carville. For me the pronouncing of words came easy, and I had fun. Surprisingly, there were very few Cajuns there, so we didn't have much need to learn French.

We took Spanish language classes from Julia Elwood. Julia was Mexican, married to a gringo. More than half the people at Carville spoke Spanish, so without Spanish, you were stuck like a pig. We told Julia she could call us "Da Kanakas." She did. And she loved the chance to hear Hawaiian spoken—although I was the only one who was fluent.

We sang for various special occasions and most of us joined the Protestant or Catholic chapel choirs. Singing quartets came from Baton Rouge, where they sometimes performed at Louisiana State University.

It seemed like I had been at Carville forever before the doctors got around to discussing my problem with the ulcer on my foot. It was later in the fall when they finally decided to cast it again. As before, the cast needed to dry for three days, and then I could walk on it. Also as before, I couldn't wait. I walked all over, and rode a bicycle. The Mexican patients all said, "Hey, you have started a bad thing." For sure it was all rough on the cast.

After a week the occupational and physical therapy people could see the cast was coming apart and they knew I would be hard on casting. By the third week, the bottom gave way and the whole cast had to be taken off. The ulcer had healed somewhat, but not completely. It was still about three-eighths of an inch across. The doctors knew that if it didn't heal, there must be something wrong in the bone. They decided to recast, hoping for healing.

After seven weeks the cast came off and voila! The ulcer was closed! The doctors thought I might be able to avoid an operation. Me, though, I was in doubt. I just knew inside me that something was wrong. It's just that so far, they had missed it. But meanwhile, it felt good to walk without the cast. I could come and go as I wanted.

Thanksgiving came soon. With the cast off, I had a lot to celebrate. There were many parties. Some patients lived off the Hansen's Disease Center's grounds, and one of them, a Filipino from Moloka'i named Paulino, invited my wife and me to his home in the town of Gonzalez about 15 miles away. His wife was Samoan, from Samoa, and they had two daughters and two sons. They came to pick us up.

We started learning about Louisiana. Carville was on the levee, and we could see ships of all sizes traveling this very long river, which seemed endless to us. We found out that Carville is legendary for its golf tournaments, drawing pros from all over.

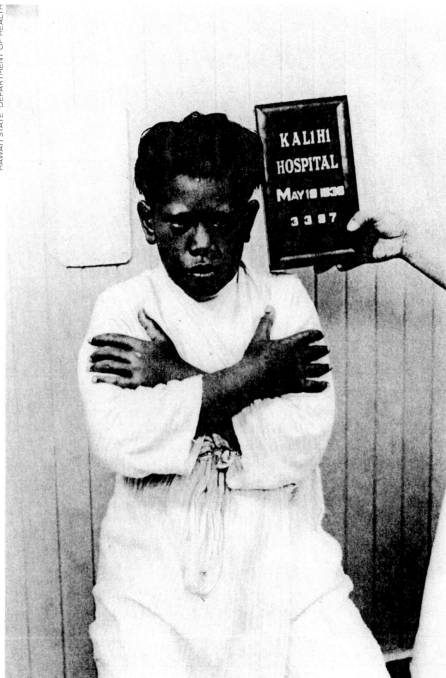

A new home: Ten-year-old Henry is admitted to Kalihi Hospital.

Henry entered the gates of Kalihi Hospital (opposite top) for the first time in 1936. Located near Honolulu Harbor (foreground, opposite bottom), the quarantine facility was a way station for many patients who would later be sent to Kalaupapa. Above, the inter-island steamship *Haleakala* approaches Kalaupapa Landing in 1924.

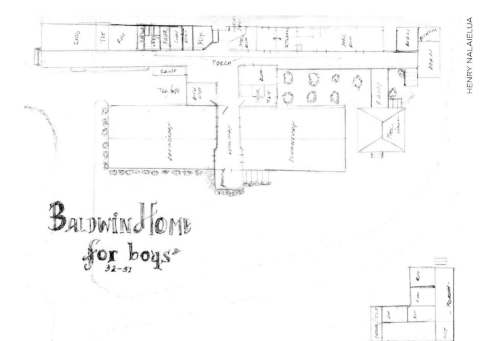

BALDWIN HOME for boys 32-51

ABOVE: A floor plan Henry recently drew from memory gives a detailed view of the second Baldwin Home, his first residence at Kalaupapa.

In the 1930s, the same building housed the police headquarters and the Social Hall at Kalaupapa.

A 1924 aerial view of the east side of the peninsula, Kalawao, shows the original Baldwin Home in the foreground and the U.S. Leprosy Investigation Center at the shoreline beyond.

ABOVE: At Kalaupapa Landing, a makeshift catamaran unloads an automobile from a ship ca. 1940.

LEFT: Henry and Tad Higa show off coconut lamps made by patients at Kalihi Hospital ca. 1940.

OPPOSITE: Henry's rendering of the mail mule at the base of Moloka'i's northern cliffs.

LEFT: Henry poses with his grandmother, Mary Waiehu Ikaika Helelā, a native Hawaiian speaker, ca. 1935.

BELOW: Henry and Sam Kaliko ca. 1958.

OPPOSITE: Henry at Kalaupapa ca. 1958; he had learned to ride a decade earlier when Moloka'i Ranch conducted roundups of free-range cattle at Kalaupapa twice each year.

The staff of the patient-published *Star* (Henry at top) stands outside the tiny office at Carville, Louisiana.

A hula dancer and Henry's *'ukulele* provide the entertainment at a party ca. 1970.

A visit with Polynesian Voyaging Society navigator Nainoa Thompson.

Henry poses with fellow Hawai'i travelers Bill Malo and Valerie Monson during one of his many trips to Belgium.

Kalaupapa Gasoline Station

1932   1986

Among the landmarks painted by Henry over the years: The old Kalaupapa gas station (above) and the U.S. Coast Guard lighthouse.

With Sally-Jo Bowman at Kalaupapa in 1995.

With Gena Sasada at Kalaupapa in 2002.

Portrait of Henry, 1995.

We crossed the Mississippi on a ferry to White Castle, a town of more than 3,000. It seemed strange to us, from islands, that a city—even these small towns—could be on both sides of a river.

Although I was in the hospital trying to heal my foot and my wife lived in House 16, she and I spent a lot of time together. Not long after we arrived, she got a job doing janitor work. Later she was employed by *The Star* to work on the address labels. And she could go wherever she wanted. Sometimes friends who had a car would take her with them to Baton Rouge.

As for me, I learned a lot about the hospital. The care was excellent. In fact, I think maybe the Hawaiians were treated even better than the rest, although I don't think anyone would admit to it.

The orderlies and nurses couldn't understand our speech, and we had a hard time with theirs. Some of it was accent, and some of it vocabulary. A lot of times, it was funny.

One stormy, rainy night Higa kept talking about "T'undah." Mrs. Wood in occupational therapy wanted to know what that was.

I explained. "Oh!" she said. "Thunder! Oh!"

Eventually I moved into House 29, a men's house. A bunch of us would play music informally—*kani ka pila*—what others called jamming. Max Gonzalez was on guitar even though no more fingers, Higa on steel guitar, and me on 'ukulele and and upright bass. No one at Carville had ever seen a bass played Hawaiian style before.

Sometimes Mrs. Harris joined us on piano. She could play just about anything, and so could I, basics to ballads, country-western, pop hits, Latin, you name it. But we stumped her with a term in Hawaiian music.

"Vamp?" she said. "What's a vamp?"

We laughed. In jazz it's improvised accompaniment. In Hawaiian music it's an instrumental line played as an introduction to a song or between verses. When we explained it, Mrs. Harris' reaction was the same as Mrs. Woods' comment on Higa's pronunciation of thunder: "Oh!"

Soon she was playing vamps right along with us. She learned fast.

At House 29-2 I lived with mostly Hawaiian guys—Sylvester, Higa,

John Deraine—and a Chinaman who had been there long before us. I was still waiting for couples housing to open up. Meanwhile, each guy had a private room and we shared a kitchen, which became a central gathering place for others as well as ourselves. Other guys from Hawai'i came from another apartment—Bernard Punikaia and Father Nobincio Fernandez, a Filipino priest from Hawai'i who was a patient. We cooked a lot, but some of the guys just hung out and drank. We could even buy beer or wine at the Carville canteen.

The only problem with the kitchen was that people would steal things from the icebox. It was a common problem at Carville—they even stole from the chapel icebox. All kinds of things disappeared from ours—two whole chickens, beer, other stuff.

I had an idea about who was doing it, and I made an open threat: "If I catch you in my icebox, you guys no going get hands."

I said "my icebox" like I owned it, which of course wasn't true, but I must have threatened the right guys, because the thievery stopped.

By October the weather was chilly. By November we were sure this place was just like Alaska. When the clothing allowance came around, we all automatically got warmer coats. We brought our own gloves.

Then, about noon on December 11, when we Hawaiians—my wife, Sylvester, Rose and Higa—were in physical therapy with Dr. Enna talking about preparing for surgery on feet and hands, someone yelled: "It's snowing!"

It was the first snow in Carville in ten years, and here it comes to the Hawaiians.

We all immediately ran out the door, leaving Dr. Enna in mid-sentence. I had been up Haleakalā and Mauna Kea, so snow was not entirely new to me. But it was to the other guys and my wife. We made snowballs and threw them at each other. It snowed all day, about three feet I think, and we made a snowman. It was worth braving the cold.

But by morning all the snow had turned to slush, and things were gooey and slippery.

We went riding out through the country. To get to White Castle we had to cross the mighty Mississippi by ferry boat to Donaldsonville, where we ate a Cajun lunch in a restaurant. It was good. I remember Lake Poulard. I thought it was huge, but I later learned that it is small compared with Lake Pontchartrain, where 2 bridges span 24 miles and a third one is 5 miles long.

Church was a big part of life at Carville. Most people belonged to the Protestant Church. The Protestants asked the Catholic Hawaiians to help them with their choir, but I was the only one who did. The Protestant minister, Oscar Harris, was a kind person who welcomed everyone as a friend. Father Jerome Kirchner was a jolly, pipe-smoking Franciscan priest who loved music. He always commented on my ability to play the upright bass viol. He insisted I must be a professional, especially because I both played AND sang.

"Nah!" I said. "Strictly amateur."

Christmas was a little sad, being away from home. But there were new things. I had eggnog for the first time. I liked it. It wasn't spiked. Of course I had sung Christmas songs in church, but this was the first time I gathered with other musicians around a Christmas tree. Some of the Louisiana people were surprised we could play Christmas music on our guitars and 'ukulele—they thought such music had to be played with violins, horns and oboes!

Then one of the Sisters of Charity came to me and said, "You're the guy who sings so well. Would you sing 'O Holy Night' for the candlelight midnight Mass on Christmas Eve?"

At the first rehearsal in the church, the choir members—18 or so— were completely surprised to hear a clear baritone. Then they joined in, along with the Sisters of Charity. For me it was such an honor, and an extreme pleasure.

On Christmas Eve the little church was full with about 75 people, both patients and staff. I'd sung "O Holy Night" many times as part of a chorus, but never the solo part. This was special, accompanied by the organ and the four-part harmony of the choir. The church acoustics were outstanding, and the place filled with the rich sound of our voices from the choir loft. I stood up so those who didn't know who I was could see me sing.

After the midnight Mass Father Jerome came to shake my hand. "Thank you so much," he said. "Thank you. That's the most beautiful rendition I ever heard. And I've never heard such a powerfully toned voice." A number of other people came to shake my hand as well.

News Year's brought the patients-only Bingo game sponsored by the patient federation, a group similar to the Kalaupapa Patient Council. It was one of six or eight games during the year. The cost—two dollars, three dollars, sometimes five dollars, was added to the jackpot for "blackout"—when you cover your whole Bingo card, instead of just B-I-N-G-O. Once I won a blackout jackpot of 89 silver dollars. I saved it until I left Carville in 1983 and gave it all to my 12-year-old niece in Hawai'i, Dandi—that is, all except 10 dollars I had exchanged when someone wanted to trade paper money for 10 of my silver dollars. I told her mother she couldn't spend it until she was 18.

About a year after our arrival, we started going to the capital city, Baton Rouge, and also New Orleans about 85 miles farther. The campus of Louisiana State University there is enormous.

Baton Rouge is not wide, but very long, with continuous shopping malls along the river. New Orleans is immense, with the glitz and splendor of endless restaurants, parks, historical places and an indoor football stadium. Between the two cities we saw all manner of boats on the river—travelers' houseboats, barges, tugs, steamboats and riverboats that go up and down the Mississippi between Louisiana and Illinois.

Mardi Gras is the big time, and the whole state looks forward to it. Fat Tuesday brings the parade from New Orleans to Beinville, a last hurrah before Lent. I saw the parade once in New Orleans.

I began to travel because of a man named Louis Boudreaux. He was the editor of *The Star,* the person who hired my wife to work on mailing labels.

I told him he looked like an "educator."

"What does an educator look like?" he asked.

I couldn't say. But for me it turned out that's just what he was.

Louis Boudreaux was a patient. He was in his early sixties, and had been at Carville 17 years. He had a fine mind. And he was blind. Yet he was able to edit the paper. He owned a car, a big one, a Pontiac station wagon. One day he called me to his office.

"Henry," he said. "I've heard you can drive."

I smiled, thinking about how I had learned by trial and error and sheer luck.

"I need a driver to take me around, especially to visit my parents in Donaldsonville. I thought about asking your wife, but I think she might get lost. Would you do it?"

I was surprised. "I'll have to think about it."

"Think hard," he said.

I remembered driving around O'ahu, especially when I was just learning my way around. I really didn't want to take the job. But the guys I hung around with all said I was missing the boat.

I went back to Boudreaux's office.

"I'll try it out," I said.

"Good."

It wasn't long before the first trip. We made a group—Sylvester, Rose, my wife, Louis and I. The driver! I was scared as hell. This wasn't Honolulu. Nothing was familiar.

Louis decided we should take the road along the river instead of Highway 61. The heavy traffic led straight into Florida Boulevard, where we went shopping and then ate at the Picadilly. It had all kinds of Southern things on the menu, but of course nothing Hawaiian. Then we headed back for Carville.

We made it back OK, but I was afraid I might get a ticket for speeding a little, or get lost. I didn't lose the panicky feeling until that big old station wagon rolled through the compound gate.

But it wasn't long before the trip began to feel like a good experience, and I was ready to go again. So was Louis. I kept the trips to town short because I didn't want to get lost. I did, though. But I never made the same mistake twice. I just used my eyesight and memory—it was years before I learned to read a map, and I never got very good at it.

The more I left the compound gates, the more Louisiana grew on me. During my second year at Carville, I joined the staff of *The Star,* working on addresses for subscriptions with my wife. *The Star* was an interesting place to be. It took two months to get everything ready for an issue, a very slow process. To me, assembling 16 pages for the old letterpress was hard work, especially when the only proofreader quit and everyone had to help.

Louis liked that I worked at *The Star*. We began to take more and more outings to Baton Rouge, and I began to enjoy being his driver. Mostly we'd go there to eat in the evening, sometimes taking other Hawaiians with us. We'd have a good time no matter what we ate—steak, Chinese, seafood, Cajun. I often had a shrimp po' boy sandwich. You no get full on that, something's wrong!

I found out Louis was Cajun, and that his wife had died. I was amazed that, despite being blind, he always knew the area we were in, Florida Boulevard, or the LSU campus. He had such a feel for the place, I guess from years of driving when he could see.

After several months of town tours he asked if I thought I could drive to his parents' place. It was 18 miles across the river, in Donaldsonville, the opposite direction from Baton Rouge.

As I did initially, I hesitated. The route was unfamiliar. And I wondered how his family would react to a Hawaiian trying to find their house.

But of course I said yes.

Donaldsonville was bigger than Kalaupapa, and bigger than my childhood hometown, Ninole, but it was still a small place. His parents owned a general store in town that was easy to find. They were semi-retired, but Louis called ahead to get them to open the store.

Until they retired, they lived above the store, but now they had a house about two miles away. We drove out there, for the first of many, many hours I would spend there.

His parents asked us to stay for a supper of shrimp gumbo and rice. We talked, and they wanted to know about Hawai'i. I told them how different we were. We talked more, and that's when I learned a secret.

Louis' last name was not Boudreaux at all. It was Houllion. In time, I would learn parts of the story of his double identity.

On that first visit, I insisted on returning early so I could find my way back. I backtracked along the same route I had come and did all right.

In time I learned that Louis Boudreaux was French—Cajun, actually—descended from the French who had come to Louisiana after being forced out of Acadia in what is now Canada's Maritime Provinces. His dad worked for the railroad in a different town, sending the children to Catholic schools. As Louis grew toward manhood, he was called to the priesthood. During his days as a young seminarian he contracted Hansen's disease. Not saying a word, he left the seminary and entered the hospital at Carville, changing his name to Boudreaux as he walked through the doors.

But it wasn't enough to shield his sister, who was still a student in Catholic school. Someone set fire to her schoolroom chair so badly it burned through the floor. Other students called her names because her brother was a leper.

Even when I was at Carville in the 1970s, patients would change their names to protect their families and themselves. Many patients buried there lie beneath headstones with no name, only a patient's number. Now it makes it very hard for relatives wanting to trace their ancestors.

We all had patient numbers, and used them regularly even with each other. But Louis was a person I have always remembered by name. Sometime after I left Carville, a person there wrote to me to tell me Louis had died.

During my third year at Carville, I was elected to the Patients' Federation Council. I thought it would be like the Kalaupapa Patients Advisory Council, a group that helped patients solve problems. I served for two terms, each a year long. By then I'd had enough of it. The problems that came to the council were mostly complaints about the hospital and the way doctors did things, or grievances with the nurses. Seldom were they important.

By this time quite a few Hawaiians had come to Carville. Some of it was because I had written a letter home and someone had posted it on a public bulletin board. Some of those who read it thought Carville sounded so good they wanted to come. Those who did come actually had a medical problem, but they mainly came to visit. Few of them stayed long. Once they arrived, they felt they didn't belong. The place was too hot, too this, too that. They thought they could run all over in the hospital but they had to stay put. A few besides me did stay—Bernard Punikaia, and Sylvester and Timothy too, but these had come before my infamous bulletin board letter. John and Olivia Breitha came, and John died at Carville and was taken home for burial.

My friends Sylvester and Rose were members of the Protestant choir. Sometimes I would join them when they needed another voice in the bass section along with Big Dennis. Dennis was a black man who had grown up in Carville, later earning a bachelor's degree in social studies at Louisiana State University and working at a women's prison. He had a fine voice. We sang many hymns, of course, but one of our favorite pieces was the Hallelujah Chorus from Handel's *Messiah*, which we sang at Christmas time. I sang with the Protestants on Tuesdays and Thursdays and with the Catholics on Wednesdays and Fridays. I was singing all the time!

Julia, the Spanish teacher, planned elaborate festivities for holidays— Easter weekend, Fourth of July, Labor Day. They all included singing. On some special occasions, a guest conductor, Mr. Toran, would come from Baton Rouge. Sometimes we traveled to the LSU campus to hear barbershop quartets from all over the region.

One year the people at Carville asked us Hawaiians to give them a taste of Hawai'i with music and food. We chose King Kamehameha Day, June 11, as the date. I thought of the bygone days when I was a young kid at Baldwin Home making a lū'au for guests from the Settlement. Like the feasts of those old days, this one took a lot of preparation. But some things would be impossible, like authentic *kalua pua'a* (baked pork). We could get the pig, and it could be roasted—but not in an underground oven. We had no taro, no banana leaf, no *imu* (earth oven) stones, junk dirt, nothing. And besides that, you dig two feet and you hit water!

About this time Sylvester, who had had tendon transplants on his hands, started talking about going home. He also revealed—after some long time keeping this hush-hush—that he had a girlfriend who was a student at LSU, Estelle Brand. Sylvester was about 30. The startling part was not their age difference, but that she was the daughter of Dr. Paul Brand, the tendon transplant man! That was big news! This was a big taboo—a romance between a patient and someone on the staff or a staff member's family. Little did I know that later I too would violate this unspoken rule.

Yet for Sylvester and Estelle, the rule went by the wayside. Her parents, both doctors at the hospital, never questioned her judgment and gave the couple their blessing. They were married soon. I did not attend because I was in the hospital again with my foot problems.

They moved to Hawai'i, where they still live at Kea'au on the Big Island.

Four great things happened while we lived at Carville. One of them was Sylvester and Estelle falling in love and getting married. Another was having Louis Boudreaux for a friend.

A third was that Marion Butler, the black guy who came to work with us at Kalaupapa doing lab tests, came to Carville to the shoe shop to learn to make custom sandals for patients whose feet had been through so much.

Dave Welch, Carville's shoe shop man, asked if I knew Butler.

"Yes," I said. "He's an OK guy."

"He's a black man," Welch said.

"I know." I was thinking about how much Hawai'i is multiracial. We're used to seeing every sort of person, and getting along with all of them. "They didn't hire the color. They hired the man."

"He'll be here in a couple of weeks," Welch said.

During my years at Carville I kept reactivating the ulcer in my foot by walking too much, and the doctors would recast the foot every so often. The drop foot was getting worse gradually too. About this time I had just come out of a cast—again—and was a good candidate for a pair of sandals. Welch asked if I would like to learn to make sandals too, so I would be able to work with Butler back at Kalaupapa.

When Butler arrived about May in 1973, I was already in the shop, taking a break from *The Star,* but still driving Louis around.

Butler knew I was at Carville, but he wasn't expecting to see me in the shoe shop. Of course he was a little older—45 or 50—but he was still the same tall, skinny guy, with those long, narrow feet—not spread out, taro patch kind feet we get.

"Eh, Henry!" He had a big smile for me, and we shook hands. "What you doing here in the shop?" Butler was from Florida, but he spoke pidgin like he'd grown up in Hawai'i.

Buddy Marchand, a shoe shop worker, came in on the middle of our conversation.

"You guys know each other?"

"Yeah," I said. "We're from the same planet." We all laughed. Then I added, "Except he get biggah foot." Butler roared with laughter.

After that, I spent every day for about three months working with Butler under Dave Welch and Buddy Marchand learning to make sandals for all those who needed them. I returned to *The Star* briefly, but Butler needed the help, and found he could work better with a Hawai'i person.

It was great working with Butler. He had such an open mind, and always did the best he could. And besides, he had been at both Kalaupapa and Hale Mohalu. We had all that in common. He was at Carville something over a year. During that time we went out to dinner several times in Baton Rouge.

Shortly before Butler left in 1974 or 1975, Louis needed my help back at the *The Star*. So I went back.

The Star finally finished moving its offices and facilities from House 16 to House 26. The staff had a lot more room, and some new equipment, including a new offset press. We had a darkroom and a paste-up room, a huge paper cutter and setter, space for the collator, and offices for the address staff, the secretary, the manager and the editor, Louis Boudreaux.

When we weren't working at *The Star,* Louis and I would go quite frequently to Baton Rouge. Now the drive was easy for me. I knew the streets, and even the stores, eateries and businesses. I got to know Donaldsonville too. Now I knew routes so well I could cross the Sunshine Bridge or I could take the small 12-car ferry near Carville. And while I was driving I would do the sightseeing, telling everything to Louis as we went. He remembered it all.

Before long we were traveling all over Louisiana, taking weekend trips to Biloxi in Mississippi, or Mobile in Alabama, even to Tallahassee, Florida. Louis would choose the routes, relying on his amazing memory. I would be the talking driver. But even blind, Louis still knew a lot more than I did. Until then I had never seen the Gulf of Mexico.

At Biloxi's harbor Louis said, "There are buildings missing."

"Oh yeah?" I said.

"Hurricane Emile," he said. It had come through in 1957. He knew all about the harbor.

On these trips we'd stay overnight in a Ramada Inn or a Holiday Inn, each paying our own way. Yes, I was doing the driving, but I wouldn't have taken his money even if he gave it to me. Money for my driving services was never a part of my friendship with Louis.

Tallahassee was an interesting old capital. We also went to Cape Canaveral, Disney World and Sea World. Louis hung onto my arm to get on the Disney World boat that went around a man-made jungle. I explained things to him as we went along. The guy ushering people onto the boat was clearly nervous about having a blind guy aboard.

"Let him go," I said. "He's fine." But the guy was a real grabber, and almost dumped Louis in the water. I took Louis by the arm and talked him into the bench seat.

Once when we were in Dallas I parked the car at the Astrodome.

"OK, Louis," I said. I wondered if he could hear me smiling. "We're at the Astrodome. You're on your own."

He stood there, hesitating, but he left the cane and depended on me.

"Come on, Louis," I said. "Walk by yourself."

He started out real slow.

Finally I said, "Eh, Louis, no worry! There's nothing here! Nothing! We're in an empty parking lot! The only building here is the Astrodome and it's still far away!" I laughed and laughed.

"Oh you," Louis laughed. "I was thinking, 'What if I run into a building?'"

Usually Sylvester or Bernard came with us. One time in Baton Rouge Sylvester was with us. He and Louis were together.

"Eh, Louis," Sylvester said. "I like shop little while. You stay here, talk to this guy? You can sit down right over here."

He parked Louis next to a mannequin. When he returned, Louis had figured it all out. He laughed. "You let a blind man talk to a dummy?" He roared with laughter.

Now and then he and I would be walking and I would say accidentally, "Turn right" when I meant left. He'd bang into something.

"What the hell did I hit?"

"A post," I said. "Sorry." And I was sorry. I didn't do these things on purpose. It's just that sometimes it was hard to remember that he was blind.

On our trips together, there we'd be, rolling along in a huge station wagon, a blind guy with a big dark man that nobody could figure out. We'd stop at a gas station or a repair garage, or a motel or restaurant, and nobody could figure out what I was—American Indian, Alaskan, Mexican or what. They never could guess "Hawaiian." I would eventually have to tell them. And then, of course, there was Louis, with his dark glasses and his cane, about 6 feet tall and about 190 pounds—my size, actually. He had white hair. He always wore a sharp white shirt and dark trousers. In short, his appearance was impressive.

Here it was spring 1973. Since we arrived in August 1972 my wife and I had been on the waiting list for a married couple apartment. Others had been on the list longer. There were only 12 apartments at Carville, plus 10 cottages, not enough for the number of patient couples. Finally we got an apartment. It had a big parlor, a bedroom, bathroom and kitchen. We both had a groceries ration and laundry service too.

But by then we were on the road to trouble, except it was one of those things you don't always see right at the time. Maybe it was the first baby, or maybe the second birth. I don't know. I remember times when she would play up to the Puerto Ricans, and times she would dance with strangers, something she never did before. Once she went out and bought new draperies we didn't need. Zap! There was 400 dollars gone! She resented the fact that I was always right and she was always wrong.

In a few months she was tired of Carville and wanted to go home. I wanted to stay. I said, "Go ahead." I had started out in Louisiana committed to being married, but by this time I could not have cared less. So in May or June of 1974, she left me in Carville and returned to Kalaupapa. We parted without a word. I knew I had no future with her, and I felt bitter.

Just like that, I was single again, a bachelor once more. I moved from the apartment back to House 29. At least now I could live my life my way. I could come and go whenever I wanted. I felt so divorced that I didn't seem to need to actually file a legal action.

Anytime Louis wanted to go out, I was available. I enjoyed those trips no matter where we went. I maintained the car—he trusted me with it, and with his Chevron charge card. I'd take it in for regular service, and got new tires when it needed them.

We went to the Astrodome in Houston to a baseball game between the Astros and the Dodgers. I had Louis walk without his cane from the Holiday Inn where we stayed. I walked ahead. When we got to parked cars, I guided him to the ticket counter.

We sat upstairs. I mean WAY up, but Louis did fine with the steps. We bought hot dogs. I watched the game, and Louis listened to it. I'd loved baseball ever since I played it as a kid at Kalaupapa. This was the big-time, especially for a country boy from Hawai'i. On our way home we went to the

Houston Space Center.

Other times we went to Dallas and San Antonio. They were both huge cities. But the place that sticks with me the most is outside of San Antonio, the Alamo. Reading about the battle there and seeing photos is one thing. But to actually walk through the place where it all happened is chicken skin. My skin tingled just thinking about all that had taken place there.

Later that summer, my wife called.

"I found somebody else," she said. "I like one divorce."

"Fine," I said. "Go get 'em." But we didn't make any arrangements or discuss the terms.

I wrote to a friend in Maryland to ask if I could visit him at Christmas. I had known Hellegaard some years earlier, when I was a police officer at Kalaupapa and he was in the U.S. Navy. He came to Kalaupapa sometimes when he was stationed in Hawai'i and we went hunting wild goats. He was out of the Navy now and living in Baltimore. I had written to him just before I left Kalaupapa for Carville. It was only July, but now I wrote again and asked if I could visit over the Christmas holidays. He said, "Come whenever you're ready."

I told Louis about my plan, and he said, "Go for it."

I would go by bus and be gone about two weeks.

But right after I made my plans, the fourth great thing about Carville happened. I already had Louis as my friend, Dave Butler had come, and Sylvester married Estelle. Those were the first three. Now a new nurse came to work at Carville. Better yet, we fell in love.

She had been born and raised in Louisiana, a true Southerner, with a strong accent. She was tall and kind of slender, pretty, with brown hair and green eyes, a few years older than my wife. From the beginning I saw that she had a warmth that overflowed. Not just with me, that's how she was.

When she came to work at Carville, I was in the hospital again, with yet another cast on my troublesome foot. She was a very outgoing person and right from the start we talked a lot, patient and nurse. Then we became friends. She offered to do my personal laundry. I agreed, but in exchange I would polish her white nurse's shoes. Soon she was pushing me around in my wheelchair and spending more and more time with me in my hospital cubicle.

One day when she was pushing me in the wheelchair, when we got to the end of the corridor she said, "Let's go for a ride."

"You going push?" I asked.

"Sure."

She stopped in another corridor. There she was, in her white uniform. There I was, in the wheelchair with my leg up to the knee in a white cast. We were alone. She walked around from the back of the chair so we could see each other.

"I love you, Henry," she said.

This was a total surprise. Like me, she was married. I did not know what to say. So I said nothing. I had to think about it, even though I knew deep down that I felt the same way.

I got out of the hospital and moved back into House 29. One day she stayed late after work. In the early evening, we rode in her truck a little way to Lake Johansson. In my pants pocket I had a pearl necklace I had bought in Hawai'i before I came to Carville. As we sat in the cab of the pickup, I pulled the little box from my pocket and put it in her hand.

"I love you too," I said. And I kissed her.

She opened the box and her eyes filled with tears.

"They're pearls," she said. "I've never seen real pearls before."

We parked there about an hour, talking then and later about ourselves. How did this happen, we both wondered? We were different racially, but that really didn't matter. If the old saying was true—"Love is blind"—then so were we.

"Is this for real?" I whispered.

She nestled against me. "Yes," she whispered back. "It is."

"Good," I said. "Because I love you." And I kissed her again.

She delivered me back to House 29 and then went home, about 45 minutes away.

Here I was, nearly 50 years old, falling in love. We both accepted this new love as real and acknowledged that it was what we both wanted. But we also both knew that neither of us was free to marry. In fact, we didn't even talk about a future together. She was still with her husband. Her oldest child, a daughter, was about to be married, but the three younger children, another girl and two boys, were still in school. Although my wife had asked me for a divorce, we had not yet filed for it.

So my darling nurse and I proceeded, day by day. I went back to work at the shoe shop. Butler was still there, and getting good at making sandals. I introduced him to Louis, and they hit it off. Soon he joined us on our outings, along with Tad Higa and some other Hawaiians. Sometimes "Lovey" would join us in our Louisiana sightseeing that fall.

As Christmastime approached, I told Lovey I had made arrangements during the summer to go to Baltimore.

"How long?" she asked.

"Only a short time."

"But how long?"

"Maybe two weeks."

"That may be short to you!" she started to cry. "But not to me! Can't you make it shorter? I'll miss you!"

"I'll miss you as much, if not more."

"Promise me you'll think of me?"

"I promise," I said.

She asked for Hellegaard's address and phone number and I gave them to her.

On Christmas Eve I sang the solo in "O Holy Night" again, with Lovey present at the midnight Mass. She spent Christmas Day with her children, and I left that day, not seeing her at all because I knew that if I did, I would not be able to make myself get on that bus in Baton Rouge.

The bus route wound through Louisiana, Mississippi, Alabama, North and South Carolina, and Washington D.C. before it got to Baltimore. The whole trip seemed longer than it was, and whether it was really four days and three nights, I am not sure. It sure felt like it.

I waited just outside the Baltimore terminal for an hour or so, bundled up and freezing cold. There was snow on the ground.

Then I heard from an area of parked cars, "Eh, kanaka! You cold?"

I smiled at Hellegaard. "Damn right, brah!" We hugged. It had been 13 or 14 years since we'd seen each other.

"You look good!" he said.

"Eh, you too!" He'd gained some weight and was balding, but it was the truth.

We drove to his home in the suburbs. Since I'd known him in Hawai'i, he had married and now had a son and a daughter who were about six and eight.

When we were corresponding a few months earlier, I had written details about things like the tendon transplant operation, which I had studied as I pondered whether I wanted it for my drop foot. It made his wife curious.

"Where did you get your education?" she asked.

At first I didn't understand why she was asking such a question. I thought about my school days so long ago at Kalaupapa and how I had told the teacher I was quitting school because my future held nothing but driving a rubbish truck.

"What?" I asked in reply.

"How did you learn all those medical things?"

Finally it came to me. "By paying attention."

"Wow," she said. "I thought you were something like a hospital intern."

I enjoyed the change of scenery, and the winter weather. There was lots of snow, and the kids made snowmen in the yard. For me it was good enough to look at it while I stayed cozy by the fireplace. I did split some wood for the fire. I hadn't done that since Kalaupapa days splitting kiawe or guava for the *imu* when we made lū'au.

Hellegaard took me touring around the D.C. area to the Lincoln and Jefferson Memorials, the Washington Monument, the White House, the Kennedy graves at Arlington and the Tomb of the Unknown Soldier. At the Naval Academy I saw a sailing ship for the first time, a square-rigger the

Navy used for training. My favorite was the Lincoln Memorial which I'd seen in schoolbook pictures, but seeing its actual size was completely impressive. It was the biggest statue I had ever seen. And yet, despite all the sights I saw, I still thought of my darling nurse, my Lovey.

I told Hellegaard I was expecting a phone call.

"Ha!" he said. "You get one wahine (woman)?"

"You got that right!"

The day after I arrived, Lovey called.

"I love you," she said. "I miss you an awful lot. More than you could ever know."

"I think I do know," I said. "I can't get you off my mind even though I'm in Maryland."

"I think I'll fly home," I said. "The bus takes too long."

"Oh, good," she said. "I love you, Henry. I miss you so much."

"I love you too. I'll be back soon."

New Year's Day 1975, only a few days after I had arrived, I caught a plane from Baltimore to Baton Rouge. It cost twice as much as a bus ticket, but I didn't care. I'd be back with Lovey so much faster.

I can't stand any good-byes, so my farewell to the Hellegaards was short and sweet. To this day I still write to them.

I got into Baton Rouge about 3 p.m., rented a car from Avis, and drove to the hospital. The next day I returned it, with Bill Wong following me so he could take me back to Carville. Bill was a fellow patient who sometimes drove for Louis. He also worked at *The Star*. Bill brought Louis with him because he couldn't find his way to the airport. Imagine, needing a blind guy along to make sure you're going the right way!

I spent that evening with Lovey.

"Lovey," I paused, thinking hard. "I want to marry you."

Tears came to her eyes. "I want to be your wife." She looked at me deliberately. "I know I'd be happy."

"We could go to Kalaupapa together," I said. But I loved her more than anything in the world, and I added, "But if need be, I could live in Louisiana with you the rest of my life."

"No," she said. "I want to come to Kalaupapa with you."

We talked of her getting a job in Kalaupapa, of what she would do with her horse. We'd stay first in Honolulu with Joseph, and decide things as we went along.

Our plans were vague, and the rest, too, was easier said than done. Our love affair had grown to this proportion, but it still was not wide open, not common knowledge.

Lovey would have to get divorced and, of course, give up her job at Carville.

I also still had to get divorced. But in addition, I still had my problem foot with yet another ulcer to heal. Besides that, I still had the drop foot, which the doctors said they could correct with a tendon transplant anytime. But I was so in love that my priorities were to get the divorce and arrange for a house at Kalaupapa. Then I would think about the transplant.

All this remained in our minds for the whole next year. For months we met at lunch. Sometimes she would stay late, after the day shift, or she would find a way to return in the evening for some program or a movie. On weekends she would come, and we'd go riding. A few times we even met in Baton Rouge.

Meanwhile, *The Star* needed me in the press room, so I left the shoe shop. I tried to learn to run the press, but it was all Greek to me, so I went back to working with the mailing labels.

With me spending most of my free time with Lovey, of course Louis didn't get to go out as often as before. One day he called me to his office at *The Star*. He was sitting at his desk. I stood across from him. His office door remained open.

"You got time for me?" he asked.

I didn't answer.

"We're not going out anymore. What's up?" He looked sad.

I hesitated. Finally I said, quietly, "I'm in love with a nurse."

"I already know that," Louis said.

I didn't reply. I was thinking, if Louis knows about this love affair, everybody in Carville knows. The place is too small to hide anything, and people do talk. I tried to think of how I should answer him.

"I know," he repeated. "It's OK. You do what is right for you. I can always find a driver, like Billy Wong."

He sounded genuine, and I knew he truly understood. I left his office with the kind of warmth you feel when things are fine.

Late in 1975 I arranged to leave for Kalaupapa in January, to take care of my divorce and arrange for housing. Lovey spent Christmas Eve at home with her family, but asked to work Christmas Day so she could be with me.

I was to leave January 20, 1976, with Timothy Waiamau, who was going home too. The night before our flight, Lovey drove with me to New Orleans and we took a room in a small hotel near the airport. She had not yet told her family about us. Instead, she had told her husband that she was going to a convention at this hotel. She expected him to call, and he did. I didn't listen, but it was a short call.

Later we made love, for the first time. It was beautiful. We slept the night through, knowing that at last we had each other, and nothing would keep us apart.

In the morning she dropped me off at the airport, where Timothy was waiting. We kissed good-bye. Then she left. I watched her drive away. She didn't even look back. I waited at the gate, ticket in hand, anxious to leave. But I missed her already, and I knew she knew it.

I had so much to accomplish—get a divorce, obtain a house, have the tendon transplant—before I could go home for good. Lovey, for some reason, would have to go to Arkansas for her divorce. But then, yes *then*, she would come to Hawai'i and we would be married.

*****

In Honolulu, Timothy and I stayed at Hale Mohalu a few days and then flew to Kalaupapa. Timothy, who had had surgery on his hands, went home to his house and I went to Bayview Home. I unpacked and jumped into shorts and a tank top. It felt great not to wear long pants. So much more comfortable. But I noticed I had turned peculiarly pale after such a long time in Louisiana.

I went to the office to see about getting a cottage at McVeigh Home.

"No more," the *kokua* (helper) said.

"Get," I said. "Cottage 13."

"Hoo, da junk," he said.

"I going fix 'em up."

"Whatevahs."

Cottage 13 had just one bedroom. It needed a lot of cleaning inside and a paint job outside. I cleaned it and got the state painter to take care of the exterior. In a couple of days it was bright, clean white, with green trim.

In three days I was ready to move in. I went to see my wife, where she was living in our old place with someone else. We didn't have much to say. She gave me some of the clothes I'd left in the house, but she wanted to keep everything else. Well, OK.

Someone gave me a table, chairs, a radio and a couple of rugs. I got a bed somewhere and borrowed some linens and blankets. I went back to Honolulu to get a small refrigerator, a washing machine and a TV set. I was ready to set up housekeeping. The only thing my new little home lacked was my darling nurse.

About this time rumors began to circulate about the possibility of Kalaupapa Settlement closing. With patients free to leave if they wanted and with no new admissions, the population was dwindling at a faster and faster rate. But what about those patients who stayed? The State of Hawai'i was still obligated to recognize and provide for us.

If it closed Kalaupapa as a Health Department facility, what would happen to the Settlement and to the land? The alternatives included the horrible possibility that a big resort would come in and obliterate all the pre-history and the history of the Settlement. Another possibility was to make the Settlement a National Historical Park.

I thought about it sometimes in the next months, during afternoons picking up Kona crab on the waterfront near the wharf with my friend

David Brede, when he got off work as a delivery man. We'd been at Baldwin Home together 30 years earlier. It was fun, pulling up the nets. I got some exercise and got my good Hawaiian color back.

Occasionally David and I would sell a few crabs. I wasn't really making any money, but then, I wasn't spending any either. If I wasn't crabbing I was just loafing around. I was confident things would work out as I had planned.

Lovey and I wrote love letters back and forth. Hers always told how much she missed me. When I'd get to thinking about it, I would feel sad and unhappy. Before long she wrote that she had lost her job at Carville because of our romance. She took another job at a nearby correctional facility for women. I knew if we kept the faith, things would turn out just fine.

My wife had done nothing about our divorce. So in June of 1977 I went to Honolulu. I already had in mind the lawyer I wanted to represent me, James Burns. He didn't think it would even be a case, and he was right. It was just a no contest divorce. I didn't even have to appear in court. All I did was pay 150 dollars, and that was that.

When I had gone to Carville, I had given away my old car to Eddie Frasco, who was a mechanic at Kalaupapa. But he wrecked it and couldn't fix it. So now I needed another car. In Honolulu I found a '74 Chev pickup that ran pretty good. It cost 750 dollars, but I had to pay the barge fee too, another 150.

With the divorce, housing and the truck taken care of, I had time to think about the tendon transplant. I understood the theory, and I knew many patients it had helped. But my big question was this: Would it work for me? Soon it was the end of the year and holiday time again. It was my first Christmas home since 1971. But I felt kind of sad, without the love of my life.

Finally, on January 26, 1977, I left for Carville for the second time. This time I was alone. And this time I wasn't just a *kua'aina*—a country boy— going on the big airplane for the first time.

When I got to New Orleans after a long night flight, I was tired. It was completely different from my first Louisiana arrival more than three years before. This time I was alone, walking off the plane with all the other passengers instead of sitting on the plane waiting to hear our names mangled over a loudspeaker. I just walked off the plane with the crowd. When the other passengers dispersed, I saw Lovey, standing alone, smiling. I smiled too, feeling really happy. She walked slowly toward me.

She looked radiant, more beautiful than ever. "Hi!" I said.

"Did you have a good flight?"

My answer had to wait while we kissed and hugged a long time. It was so good to see her at last.

While I picked up my baggage, Lovey went for her car. I loaded my bags and we were bound for home. It took about an hour to reach the cottage she had rented in Gonzalez about a year earlier. By now she had separated from her husband and all of her children were gone.

Like the place I had in Kalaupapa, this cottage was white with green trim. The small back yard was fenced. Everything was in good repair. The place was small, two bedrooms, parlor, bathroom and kitchen. It was cozy. In fact, totally comfortable.

"This is just big enough for two," I said.

"Uh huh," she said. And kissed me again.

I had planned to make a Chinese dinner, so we went to buy the groceries. Lovey had invited my old friend Bernard Punikaia, and a new Kalaupapa patient now at Carville, Norbert Palea. I had known him years ago at Baldwin Home. He was paroled about the same time I was, around 1949. Most of the other Hawaiians at Carville had gone home. Norbert and Bernard were among the few left. But they didn't show for dinner, and Lovey's brother and her younger daughter, Jean, came an hour late. After they left we cleaned up the kitchen.

It was a chilly winter night. When we went to bed we doubled the blankets and spent a warm and cozy night in bed, the first in a year. It was beautiful.

The next day I went to Carville and conferred with Dr. Enna and Dr. Brand about the tendon transplant. It would be a long-term investment of sorts, and it was not without risk. It would take a year before Dr. Enna would know for sure if it was successful. At first I asked him for more time. But then I decided, "The sooner, the better." I'd have the operation in three days.

Lovey took time off from her job at the prison until then. I remember going to the levee in Baton Rouge with her after my doctors' conference. It was a picturesque place, with trees flowering already, even in the nippy weather. We talked about the operation, about our future together; we had lunch at Emile's, a favorite seafood restaurant. Then we drove across the Sunshine Bridge through Gonzalez to Thibodeaux, where her daughter and her doctor husband lived.

Soon the doctor came home from work, greeting us cordially and inviting us to join them for dinner at a restaurant. So we went out again. The whole evening was comfortable. In fact, Lovey's son-in-law was a great guy. We had such a good time it turned into a late evening. We didn't get home until about 11:30 p.m.

My three days with Lovey in our new house went by all too fast. Then she drove me to Carville and I entered the hospital, where it took about a week to get me ready for the surgery.

Tendon transplants had been quite successful with patients whose hands were "crabbed" or who had cerebral palsy. The surgery also often helped "drop foot" such as I had, which is caused by paralysis. The doctors take the Achilles tendon and join it to the tendon that moves the foot up and down. My hope was to be able to walk normally again.

The operation was on a Thursday. Lovey would return to work later on the night shift at her job, but she prepped me for surgery at 9 a.m. Within half an hour I was wheeled into surgery and was out cold. Next thing I knew, I woke up. It was about five hours later. I was groggy as hell and went right back to sleep. When I got up again, it was about 5:30 p.m. and I was very hungry. I was flat on my back and in a lot of pain. It was still hours before Lovey's night shift, and she came to feed me.

Dr. Enna estimated the recovery time at six weeks. But that did not count additional time for exercising and retraining my foot to work again. It would actually be two and a half months, the longest time I ever spent healing any part of my body. Many times in the past I had had to be patient, but this required even more learning to endure.

This time, I could feel pain in the whole foot. When it subsided after about two weeks, I had time on my hands. The foot was not in a cast, but I was confined to a wheelchair. Lovey came whenever she wasn't working, pushing me in the chair like the time she first told me she loved me.

I asked her to buy me a 24 by 36 inch canvas. I set up the canvas and my oil paints in my hospital room and began a painting of St. Philomena's, Father Damien's church back at Kalaupapa.

In my time at Carville, yet another problem common among patients worsened. Nerve and blood vessel damage from Hansen's disease can cause trouble with the feet and hands. Feet cripple, or the fingers may claw. Years earlier, at Kalaupapa, the fingers of my left hand had started to curl a little, just the tips. Then I noticed that I couldn't straighten my fingers out flat. Slowly, slowly this proceeded to the second knuckle, the fingers curling over toward the palm of the hand. By the time I got to Carville, I really had "crab hands."

Having these hands, maybe you're handicapped. Some people have tendon surgery. Some even lose their fingers. I am—lucky is not the right word —fortunate. These hands never prevented me from drawing or painting, or playing the 'ukulele.

For the painting, I was working from a black and white photo that had run on the cover of *The Star*. Little by little the painting took shape. Nurses and orderlies asked questions. What are you painting? Is it Carville? Or somewhere else? Are you going to sell it? To judge from these questions, my "crab hands" weren't hampering me.

I didn't really have a purpose for the artwork. Mostly I was just killing time.

I finished the painting in about a month, a little before *The Star* moved into its new quarters in House 26. The publication would have a lot more space and equipment for the new photo offset process, including a new press that would be three times faster than the old one. There would be a dark room, a computer room for the address plates, a pasteup room, and offices for the editors and proofreaders. And there was a room for the memorabilia of *The Star*'s founder, Stanley Stein.

The Star opened its new offices with a lot of hoopla. I took my painting over to Louis Boudreaux's office, carrying it about 75 yards via wheelchair. He was quite surprised. He'd thought a lot about art, and I could tell he was pleased.

The carpenters knew I was coming, and had put up hangers for the painting on the wall behind Louis' desk. I told him how good the painting looked there.

Then I said, "If I die before you, you keep the painting. If you die first, I will take it back."

"OK by me," he said. "I appreciate your hanging the picture in my office."

Louis passed on not long after I returned to Kalaupapa in 1982, and I got the painting back about a year later. I hung it in my home in Kalaupapa. Just recently, in 2003, the painting was part of my first one-man show, at Native Books in Honolulu. By the second week of March, although I was still in the hospital, I was able to go back to work at *The Star,* doing mostly menial tasks.

My foot had healed and I was walking right for the first time since 1972! I still had some pain, and I certainly couldn't run, but the miracle was I could walk without tripping over myself. I think the success of this surgery depends not only on the doctors knowing what they are doing but on the patients themselves believing in the operation. I had believed in it from the start.

When I was released from the hospital I went back to live with Lovey in the cottage in Gonzalez. I kept working at *The Star*. At first, she would drop me off and pick me up. Then I bought a second-hand pickup, and transportation was easier for both of us. But several months later, on my way to work, I got rear-ended while I was at a stop light. In a week I was over the resulting backache and neck pains, but the truck was a total wreck and I bought another one, a '75 Chevy.

The Star's new photo offset system required camera work and pasteup. I "graduated" to doing pasteup, which I enjoyed. The staff added a professional writer. Her husband was the hospital photographer who also did some work for *The Star*. Because of these additions, the magazine became first-class, and we could see it. It made us proud of the publication, and of ourselves. Unfortunately, they only stayed about a year and a half. After that *The Star* began to lag.

Now we used the new pickup for weekend trips. Sometimes I still took Louis out too, enjoying our enduring friendship. We saw each other every day at *The Star* as well.

Many of the trips Lovey and I took were spur-of-the-moment, in Arkansas and Oklahoma as well as Louisiana. One trip was to Pensacola, Florida, to meet a friend of mine in the Navy on the USS *Saratoga*. We went to Mexico in June of 1977, crossing the border at Eagle Pass, Texas. In the border office where we did the paper work, an armed guard on the Mexican side asked where our car was parked. I walked with him to Lovey's Volkswagen while she finished the documents. The Spanish I had learned earlier at Carville now paid off.

"What's your name?" I asked in Spanish.

"Roberto. *Como se yama usted*?"

"*Mi me yamo Enrique*," I replied.

Roberto smiled.

He looked inside the car and saw our suitcases on the back seat but made no move to open them.

"Aren't you going to look in our suitcases?" I asked.

"Enrique," he said. "I trust you. No need to open the bags."

"*Gracias*," I said, and tipped him. He left. I waited at the car for Lovey.

"Did he search our car yet?" she asked.

"No," I said. "When I spoke to him in Spanish, he decided he didn't need to."

"Really! They always search the bags." In times past, she had been searched and it wasn't fun.

On foot we crossed the bridge over the Rio Grande into Piedras Negras, Mexico. Immediately we saw a huge array of beggars, most of them children, some of them drunk men and some young girls prostituting themselves. She wanted to go to a particular Mexican clinic to get some medicine for an acquaintance that was not available in the United States. We stayed a night in El Hotel Aguila. On our way back, we bought a huge papaya, which we had with us crossing back to the American side of the border. We showed it to the American border guard and he smiled. We took it back to our hotel and ate it all.

It was time to head home. We drove toward San Antonio, heading for the Alamo. We loaded the camera and both took a lot of pictures, a few of each other, but mostly of the place. Once again I was profoundly affected by being at this famous landmark, this mighty "little frontier" where brave Americans stood and fought to the last man against the endless armies of Santa Anna so freedom might prevail. The hallowed place is a living tribute to a group of unsung heroes fighting for freedom.

East from San Antonio we saw a sign for "New Braunfels" at about lunch time, so we headed there. It turned out to be a little German settlement. We chose a restaurant because it had numerous cars parked outside, and entered a beer garden. The menu was a mystery, so we asked the waitress what was popular. Our lunch was sauerkraut and sausage, and a huge pitcher of beer, which came with it. We asked for a smaller pitcher, but they served only the giant size. We didn't like the beer much, but the lunch was good.

Later that year, I bought a brand new '77 white Chevy pickup. But my luck with trucks wasn't any better than it ever had been. Before I had owned it a year, some woman ran a stop sign and rammed the front end while I was driving. The only injury was that Lovey banged the bridge of her nose on the dashboard. But the front end of the car that hit us was demolished. My new truck wasn't totaled but the front end was such a mess I used the insurance money to buy yet another new pickup, this time a red Chevy.

Time just rolled along, with work during the week and trips on the weekends. We were happy in the little cottage, and I was never once sorry for being in Louisiana. It had provided a solution to all my troubles with my foot. I had met my great and good friend Louis. And my darling nurse.

But by 1982 it had been ten years since I first came to Carville and I wanted to go home. Most of the Hawai'i guys who had been at Carville had already left. I wanted to go back to the plan we had made in 1976, to return to the place I had arranged in Kalaupapa, and to get married. She agreed.

"1983," I said.

So, in 1982 she took me to the airport, again. Again I arrived in Honolulu, stayed at Hale Mohalu overnight, and flew on to Kalaupapa. My neighbor Frasco picked me up. I got off at my cottage, unloaded my stuff, said hello to Frasco's wife, Gertrude. They asked me to join them for supper.

Lovey called. As always, she cried. She missed me terribly. I told her I was fine and everything was OK. She said she was ready to make her trip to Arkansas to get the divorce. Why she had waited so long I do not know. I never asked. She told me she might be gone a few days, but she would call as soon as she got home.

I waited for her call. It came two days later. I had never asked questions about her divorce, but I was glad now to know it was final. Likewise, she didn't ask about mine. There are some things better left alone.

But now we were both divorced. Our new life was about to begin.

Home of My Heart

CHAPTER 7

Kalaupapa 1983

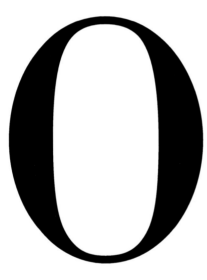

On January 23, 1983, I waited at the Honolulu Airport. I was an hour early. I checked the flight number and the gate. The plane was late. I had coffee and read the morning paper. Finally, I went to where Lovey would get off the Wiki Wiki bus airport trolley. I was still early. And anxious. Even when the plane landed, it took quite some time for passengers to disembark. Finally bunches of them came on the trolley. I watched them come off both the front and middle doors of the trolley.

No Lovey. I began to worry. Where could she be?

"Is there another trolley? My wife should be here already," I asked the driver.

"Oh yeah," she said. "A full load. Don't panic. She'll be on the next one."

But she wasn't. Now what? I went to the arrival desk. Yes, she was listed on the flight.

My only other idea was to go the baggage claim. There she was, in the waiting area.

What a relief!

I hugged her, and kissed her hard and long. "How did you get off the trolley without me seeing you?"

"What trolley?" she said. "I got off the plane with a bunch of Louisiana basketball players and walked down the stairs with them. When I didn't see you right away, I knew all I had to do was wait, and you'd find me."

"Well, you had me scared for awhile. I'm sure glad I finally found you." I kissed her again.

I had taken a room at a hotel because I knew she would be tired after the long flight. We went out for a light supper, talked some, and then I called Joseph. I told him about Lovey, and asked if we could come over tomorrow and stay for a few days.

"Sure," he said. "You're full of surprises, aren't you?"

The next day we went to his house early enough to all go out to breakfast. Joseph and Lovey hit it off like two peas in a pod.

Later I called Sister Wilma, the director of nursing at Kalaupapa, and Lovey talked to her about a possible position. Lovey had outstanding credentials and, fortunately, there was an opening that would be available by the time she got her license from the Department of Health. Then we went to the state DOH offices to fill out her application, and to the federal building for her to apply there, as a back up.

In two or three days she had her nursing license and we were done in Honolulu. I made a one-way reservation to fly to Kalaupapa. We got on the plane and were there in half an hour. I left her at the little airport, went to get the truck, came back, loaded our luggage, and drove to my cottage at McVeigh. It wasn't the one I had fixed up earlier, but practically identical. I unloaded our baggage and we walked inside. At last we were home.

We sat on the bed and kissed for a long, long time.

"It reminds me of our home in Gonzalez," she said. Indeed it did, a small cottage, white with green trim, a small yard.

We visited the neighbors, returning to our cottage about 8:30 p.m. Our first night at home was ecstatic, and we slept like two cooing doves.

I got up at 4:30 a.m. and went to the hospital, where I had been doing janitorial work since I had returned to Kalaupapa alone. At 6:30 I went home to get Lovey, so she could begin with the morning shift at 7 a.m.

By the end of the week, we were talking marriage. In April we decided on our wedding. It would be on a Wednesday, her day off. I asked her what kind of wedding she wanted.

"Simple," she said.

"I'm with you."

I made arrangements with the *kahu* (minister) at Kana'ana Hou Protestant Church. Lovey put on a simple dress, nice, but nothing fancy. I traded shorts for white trousers and a green aloha shirt. I had neglected to provide witnesses, so outside the church I grabbed a patient off the street, William Ka'akimaka. Nearby, in the post office, I found another patient, Sarah Benjamin.

"Where we going?" Sarah asked as I hustled her toward the church.

"Kana'ana Hou," I said.

"What we doing here?" William asked.

"We getting married," I said. "We need witness."

At the same time they both said, "We not dressed right!"

"You'll be just fine," I said.

They muttered a little more protest, but then we all went into the church, where the four of us stood before the altar and the *kahu*. The ceremony was over in just a few minutes. We promised "Til death us do part," the *kahu* pronounced us man and wife, and I kissed the bride.

We were now Mr. and Mrs. Nalaielua! Benjamin and Sarah shook our hands and they walked back to whatever we had interrupted with our wedding.

We went home, changed clothes, had some lunch, and sat on our porch. I felt all warm inside. At last I was married to my darling nurse!

Lovey was in love with me and with Kalaupapa, the blue of the ocean, the lush green of the land. At first she couldn't believe she could walk in the forest and not see snakes. I told her, not only that, we didn't have any number of other Louisiana creatures either—skunks, bears, 'gators, pumas, wild turkeys. Soon she was walking everywhere, although she did carry my .22 rifle just in case.

In Louisiana she had hunted ducks now and then with her son. I'd hunted for years, deer, pig and goat. Now it was her turn. The first time I took her out, we didn't see anything. The next time, on her day off, I gave her the "big" gun, a .30-06 rifle. She went alone along a dry river bed. I was to meet her later with the truck. She shot a small axis buck, her first.

"*Auwe* (too bad)," I said when I saw it. "We can't clean it. You shot its guts to pieces."

She looked puzzled. "See?" I said, slitting open the deer. The whole stomach area was smashed. "There's no good meat. You're gonna have to do better than this."

We hunted every now and then, sometimes seeing herds of deer, but they would run. One day, on the east end of the peninsula at Kalawao, I said, "Go see what you can do. Then we'll have some deer meat to eat."

She found a large buck away from the herd. This time she dropped the deer with one shot to the head.

"Wow," I said. "That was good."

"It's not my first time," she said. "I hunted white-tailed deer in Louisiana."

I put the buck over a large rock and gutted it, then put it in the pickup and took it home to skin it. We shared the meat with neighbors and kept some for ourselves.

She liked the beach, and the deep ocean too, often remarking on the dark blue of the deep water off Kalawao and the green of the shallows on the other side. She could swim and wanted to learn to dive—but *auwe*! Her *'ōkole* (butt) came up and she couldn't sink!

I'd been on the waiting list for a house for quite some time, and later in 1983 one opened up—the same house I still have. It has two bedrooms and a very large parlor, and a kitchen and a bathroom, of course. It was about twice the size of the cottage. Outside, the place had a little carport and a gigantic yard with three mango trees and a lychee tree.

Occasionally we'd go to Honolulu to shop, staying with Joseph in his house in Waimalu. We'd go out for breakfast and supper—his treat, because he liked Lovey so much. She ordered whatever she thought she would like. She liked Chinese food, but not Japanese, although she tried to acquire a taste for it. Her favorite items were pastries and Portuguese sausage.

Once Joseph said to me, "She talk funny kine."

"That's how they speak in Louisiana," I said, smiling. "Funny kine."

We visited Robert and Nani too, and Lovey met my baby girl. By then she had graduated from high school in Pearl City and was working, although she still lived at home. Robert had told her some time earlier about the adoption, so she knew I was her father. Things seemed a little easier than when she was very young.

She greeted us both with a kiss. I had been "Uncle Henry" from day one and I still was. Now she called my wife "Aunty." She sat down with us, visiting easily and comfortably.

During this time, Kalaupapa had become a National Historical Park. In 1984, the first superintendent, Henry Law, came to begin the creation of the park. The Hawai'i Department of Health continued to administer the Settlement, and would until no patients needed assistance. The State Department of Hawaiian Home Lands, which controls some of the acreage, also has an administrative role.

Within six months things began to happen, particularly the gathering of artifacts. The old jail, where I'd put a few drunks to sleep it off, became the repository of old things people donated or that had come from places that were shut down, like Bayview Home's pool hall that was used to store old clothing, radios, utensils, unclaimed things from people's estates, the Japanese Society's Shinto club house, even the hospital lab, where they found fumigation medicines, logs, record books and maps.

In 1988, after four years as the National Park Superintendent, Henry Law left for a more prestigious assignment with the Park Service. We didn't know it then, but that is a pattern in the Park Service. Now we found out that the Park Service people are on assignment—brief assignment. Nobody wants to be the superintendent of such a small park forever. In a word, the superintendents like to be promoted. At times it made a problem for us. but it's still better to be a National Park than not. The park is basically a good thing, and maybe the only way for Kalaupapa to remain a historical place so people can learn and know about all that happened here. We wanted it to be a way of preserving our *mana'o*—our thoughts and feelings and insights gained from living here for decades, and from knowing about the decades that preceded us.

I had been a member of the Patient Advisory Council off and on since sometime in the sixties. I joined because I thought I could learn something and perhaps become a leader. The main thing I learned was that all the members were real hard heads, including yours truly. The kinds of patient issues that came up before the council were largely complaints about things like speeding tickets, the waiting list to get one of the Settlement houses instead of living in McVeigh, Bishop or Bayview Homes, or the ration system for those living in the cottages. It became tiresome hearing these problems, yet I still served two decades on.

About this time, 1985, when I was the Council secretary, Bernard Punikaia resigned from the State Board of Health after serving several years. The rest of the members of the Council asked me to take his place. I said no. I couldn't be as good as Bernard had been. He had been a member of the Patient Council for years, and had refined his natural knack for knowing what to say and when, a talent I still lack. Bernard had been a fighter from the beginning, maybe even before he came to Kalaupapa from Kalihi Hospital in 1942, a few months after I had. He was not afraid of anything. But he knew to listen, and to learn from it. He didn't finish his high school diploma until he was at Carville with me in the early seventies, but he was naturally articulate. When he represented anyone at the Patient Council, the Board of Health, or anywhere, you couldn't beat him.

I couldn't match that kind of show and I said so. But the Patient Council still thought otherwise and submitted my name. Now I have been appointed or reappointed by all the governors since George Ariyoshi. I'm still on the

Board, even though in recent years I have been unable to attend meetings.

One thing like this leads to another. The Patient Council asked me to serve on the Moloka'i Burial Council, which dealt with the Hawaiian remains that turned up every once in awhile, particularly at the beginning of construction projects. I declined. I didn't want to be on it. I didn't know anything, and I said so. But I was chosen.

In the summer of 1985 Lovey and I took a trip to the mainland to visit her family. We flew into Dallas-Fort Worth, where her youngest son worked at the airport. We met her brother, then picked up our rental car and went to her son's apartment. They all wanted to talk story, but I went to bed. After two or three days, it was time to visit her older son, who lived in Benton, Arkansas. We stayed several days.

Back in Lousiana, we stayed overnight with her daughter and her husband. As usual, we arrived late at night. They lived in Gonzalez in the same house we had rented. It felt nice to be home in Gonzalez, but I was so tired I had to go to bed while the rest of them stayed up and talked.

Because we stayed a week, I had time to go visit Carville. The place had changed a lot. It wasn't so active, and a lot of staff had either left or retired. It was nice to see the few oldtimers still there. Then we drove back to Dallas-Fort Worth and flew back to Honolulu, stayed a few days with Joseph, and then caught the Kalaupapa plane for home.

We settled into our house again, and the very next day Lovey went back to the day shift shift at the hospital at 7 a.m. The whole trip had been great, and I felt as much in love as ever.

I was doing part-time janitor work in the early mornings and driving tours of our peninsula for Ike's Scenic Tours from about 10 a.m. until 2:30 p.m.

After her shift, Lovey would sometimes hike up to Kauhakō Crater, about three miles. If I wasn't hunting pig, I'd be cleaning our yard, mowing, weeding, raking leaves from under the trees.

Some evenings we'd hunt deer or wild pig with our two dogs, a tan Lab and a white Bull Terrier. The Lab would corner a pig. I usually shot it, or sometimes, if it was a small pig, the terrier would make the kill. That dog was never scared, even if the pig was bigger than he was. My neighbor loved pig meat and would cook it, then give me some. Lovey tried it but didn't like it.

We both loved those afternoons visiting the beach and evenings hunting in the green valleys. We were truly happy.

*****

Late in 1985 the same old foot with the same old ulcer started acting up again. I'd had the foot trouble ever since Boy Scout days, when I was running around barefoot in Waikolu Valley and accidentally stepped on that broken guava stick. Then it was only a little hole, a half-inch circle. But in 40 years, it took a huge toll.

The problem is, because of nerve damage from Hansen's disease, there's no feeling in the foot, so I don't feel what's going on. It's common among patients. A sore opens. Unattended, it gets infected. It might heal in three to six months as a callus grows around it—but the sore remains underneath, waiting to act up, to break down from inside. Improper shoes make it worse—and you don't even have to walk very far to get in trouble. Going barefoot is dangerous too. As kids, we were reminded to constantly check our feet. But of course we didn't, and by the time we noticed something wrong, it was too late and we had a major problem. One of the worst things is that, in general, foot ulcers get worse with each recurrence as you get older.

Lovey didn't monitor my foot because the hospital had a special dressing nurse, and a doctor who visited once a week. I had my foot dressed every morning at the hospital, and I did it again myself every night. Yet it got worse.

The foot needed surgery again, so I went to Hale Mohalu in late 1985. The surgery was done at Queen's Medical Center. The idea was to remove all the dead skin around the ulcer as well as a sharp bone protrusion, and so flatten the ulcer. This time there would be no cast, and I would have to have complete bed rest at Hale Mohalu for the entire convalescence. The doctors thought it would be about six weeks. It actually took longer than six months.

Lovey came to visit me two or three times, but it was hard for her, not knowing the streets in Honolulu. I told her it was all right to go home, maybe come just now and then.

After months without a visit, I called home. No answer. I called many evenings, but still no answer. It seemed odd, especially day after day. Where was she? She got off work in the middle of the afternoon, so I knew she wasn't at work. It began to seem odd, too, that she hadn't visited me in such a long time.

Then one time I called and she answered.

"I've been calling every evening for days," I said. "Where you been?"

"Out riding." Her voice was edgy. She didn't say anything more.

By her tone of voice, I knew what was going on, and reached my own conclusion. But I didn't say anything.

The ulcer was somewhat healed. I told the doctors I better go home. It was July 1986.

I called Lovey to tell her to expect me, but when I got to the airport at Kalaupapa she wasn't there. She showed up after about 20 minutes. She didn't even kiss me. I knew I was right. Something was very wrong.

She had houseguests from the Big Island, but they left the next day, a Sunday. For the whole next week I felt like I was getting the cold shoulder, not unlike the situation years before with my first wife. I noticed that a man would come by the house several times a day. But he could see I was home and he didn't stop. Sometimes Lovey would go off alone on her bicycle, leaving me at home. My foot was healed enough that I could walk around a little and drive, but I knew I should be careful—not just about the foot, but because I was thinking to myself, "Something is up and it's going to come."

The next Saturday night I came back from taking a short ride in my truck. Lovey was sitting at the dining room table. I had already had supper, but I came and sat down on a chair.

She did not look at me, but out the window instead. She said, "Henry, I'm in love with another man."

I'd had my hunch, but I sat there in total shock. I couldn't say a thing.

"I'm moving out as soon as possible. I'm sorry. Henry, I don't love you anymore."

In my head I was saying to myself, "Be calm, this is not happening, she didn't say it, you heard wrong."

But I did hear her, loud and clear. She had said, "Henry, I don't love you anymore."

The idea of divorce hit me like a boulder. I felt like I was about to commit a crime, I was so angry. The hurt was so overwhelming I wanted to strike out at her, but that's not what I am made of. I just sat there, and somehow sanity prevailed.

I went to bed, but the night wore on. I don't know where she was. Finally tears came, and I slept a little. On Sunday morning she left. She returned Monday for her nurse's uniforms. Tuesday she came to ask for one of the cars. I gave her the sedan and kept the truck.

And that was it. I was all alone with a big empty hole in my heart and an empty house. No one to come home to, no one to hold. Nothing.

"Henry, I don't love you anymore." Six words. A short sentence. Swift but sure, no "maybe" about it. No big ruckus, no screaming and yelling. She was determined to go, and that was that.

I tried to repair the hurt by going out every night riding by myself, staying out late, trying to clear my head enough to cope with the sudden emptiness. But mostly I just endured the passing days, weeks and months, trying not to look back. We'd been together 12 years.

I didn't see her again until one morning when she showed up with divorce papers. I was raking leaves in the yard. She stopped her car, got out and walked toward me. I walked toward the car. She handed me a pen and I signed the papers she held out. Not a word was said. As I signed, I thought, "Good riddance." But I didn't really mean it.

It was 1986. My brother Joseph, with whom I had lived so many times in Honolulu, had become diabetic, dying in a care home. As a veteran of World War II, he was buried in the National Memorial Cemetery of the Pacific.

My oldest, closest brother had died. My wife had left me. I was 60 years old and I knew I had to live my life alone.

The summer of 1986 brought the surprise of another divorce. Later that year I was invited to join the Kupuna Program with the Office of Hawaiian Affairs, particularly to help the effort to continue the Hawaiian language. The organizers wanted me to share my *mana'o* as an elder in the Hawaiian community as well as speak Hawaiian. Through the program, I was invited to a long weekend gathering of photographers at a Waikīkī hotel. I brought old photos of Kalaupapa and also some slides. Some of them I had taken, and some of them were part of the collection of the Kalaupapa Historical Society. No one had seen such photos and I was the hit of the meeting.

After the meeting I talked to a very friendly haole woman named Janie, a receptionist who had registered everyone for the conference. I had a car and offered her a ride home, but she said no. And that was that. But I did think she seemed like a good woman.

Later, after I'd been back at Kalaupapa for a while, I received a surprise —a card from Janie inviting me to a Christmas party at her apartment in Honolulu. I accepted and flew to Honolulu. It was a Friday. She lived on Liliha Street with her daughter. The party included about 15 people. By midnight everyone but Janie's sister and I had left. We helped clean up, and then Janie asked if I could drive her sister home. Janie came with us. Then I returned Janie to her apartment and she asked if I would like to stay overnight. I slept on the couch in the parlor, in my clothes. The next day I went to where I was supposed to be staying, the cottage at Leahi Hospital that was set aside for use by Kalaupapa patients visiting Honolulu. It was a spacious two-story building with a kitchen, two bathrooms, and ten individual rooms.

Later I called Janie and asked her out to dinner and a movie. Afterward we went to her place. I stayed awhile. And I took her in my arms and held her. Then we talked for awhile.

I stood up. "I don't want to spoil the hospitality," I said. She hugged me. "Can I come again?"

"Yes," she said, hugging more. I kissed her—and went out the door, to the cottage in Kaimukī.

I was to return home the next day, Sunday, but first I went to her house. "I'm going home to Kalaupapa," I told her. "I hope you'll come to visit me."

"Oh yes," she said.

"You have my phone number." I kissed her good-bye. "Call me."

I went to catch the plane home. It had been some Christmas weekend!

After exchanging some letters and a few phone calls, Janie came to visit for a long weekend. It was her first ride in a small plane—a big adventure for her. I took her home to my house. We sat in the parlor.

"Your house is so clean," she commented. "You must have a maid, or a cleaning woman."

I laughed. "No such thing! When you live alone you do what you have to do. Like your own chores."

I took her for a ride through the Kalaupapa village, then out by the lighthouse and down to the beach, where she took some pictures.

She stayed at my house three days, but said she'd like to come back to stay longer. She flew back to Honolulu, but that night she called. This was starting to feel like love. I was almost forgetting that I had resigned myself to living the rest of my life alone.

In about two weeks she called again, asking if she could come back and this time bring her son with her. He was visiting from the mainland, where he lived with his father. Her daughter was away in Florida.

"How old is he?" I asked.

"Seventeen. Is there a problem with that?"

"No."

A month later they came for a week. As soon as they got off the plane, the kid, Daniel, wanted to go to the beach.

"Whoa!" I said. "We go get settled first. Then we'll see about the beach."

I took them home to my house. They put their suitcases in the spare bedroom.

"You hungry?" I asked.

"No, thank you."

"Well then. Let's go!"

At the beach Daniel explored every little nook and cranny, running over rocks, chasing black crabs, looking for coral. Janie and I just sat on the sand and watched him enjoying himself. It didn't seem to matter to him that he was alone.

"He's never been to a place like this ever," Janie said. "I wanted him to see what it is like to be in a place that is not crowded with people. I thought it would be a really good thing for him."

She was right. I took them on a tour. Daniel had more questions than a newspaper reporter. Whenever we got out of the truck, he was cautious but not afraid. He couldn't get over the mountains and cliffs being so close.

We took a picnic to a black sand beach at Kalawao. Another day Daniel swam at Papaloa Beach.

"Henry!" The kid said. "Aren't you going to swim with me?"

"Nope."

"Come on. Please?"

"I live here," I said. "I can swim any time, any day." I didn't know how to explain that the eternal ulcer under my left foot prohibited me from swimming.

He looked at the waves. "I wish I could live here," he said.

Janie saw a change in her boy from the first day. "He'll never forget this," she said. "Or you."

"Oh, he will, in time. Once he's grown up, it will all wash over him."

After a week, we put the kid on the plane for Honolulu. Janie stayed a few more days. She wanted me to take her on the tour again, but this time she would tape record all that I said. She wasn't a writer or reporter.

"You have so much knowledge," she said. "I doubt there's more than two people who can tell the story of Kalaupapa and Kalawao so well. If I record you, this way more people can hear you." I'm sorry to say, I don't know what became of the tapes.

When she left, I went with her. In Honolulu we'd go to a movie, or out to dinner. I'd return to Kalaupapa. She'd come visit again. On her last trip to Kalaupapa we drove up to the top of Kauhakō Crater and bumped into my second wife, who was walking. She stopped, and I introduced her and Janie.

That night Janie and I had a serious talk about whether we had a future together. Could we live as one? Could we make it? Was it something we both wanted?

More questions arose. Where would we live? Where would she work? If it were to be at Kalaupapa, could she leave her present life?

Ultimately, life together was not to be. I did not want to leave Kalaupapa. Janie felt Kalaupapa would shut her in.

I listened to her words, and agreed with her. I certainly didn't want to force her to do anything against her will. And so it was. I took her to the airport the next day. We kissed good-bye. And she was off and gone.

Even though I had enjoyed my months with Janie and I thought that I had loved her, this decision settled easily inside me. This time, for some reason, instead of feeling abandoned or deceived again, I felt all right that we wouldn't be together forever. Maybe what we had shared was infatuation. Or friendship. Or just a few months of good times. I felt there would be more good times with other people.

Janie did write several months later to tell me she had met a man with three children and was going to marry him. After they got married, they took off for the mainland and that's the last I heard from her. I wrote to her, wishing her the best. I never heard from her again.

The latter part of 1987 brought a new opportunity that led me to a much better understanding of all of Kalaupapa. I went to work for another patient, Isaac Keao, as a guide for Ike's Scenic Tours. Later, when Ike went out of business, I guided for Gloria and Richard Marks' Damien Tours.

I had been doing janitorial service at the hospital since 1983. Isaac's tours had been increasing in demand, and he needed a third driver. He asked me. Soon I became a full-time employee, guiding a tour for about four hours each day.

At first I thought, "Hah! That's easy! How much is there to learn about

Kalaupapa? There's a limit to this place." But I was to become more aware of a lot of things I hadn't known and had never considered. One of these was the history of the peninsula before King Kamehameha V selected it in 1863 to be the quarantine facility for people afflicted with the leprosy that seemed to be an epidemic in the Hawaiian Kingdom, a disease that no one understood much at all but that frightened a great many people.

The disease, it turns out, is only a recent development on this peninsula. Hawaiian people lived here for centuries before the Kingdom started its first health department Settlement at Kalawao. I learned that, from the coastal region in the lighthouse area you can still see clearly some of the rock wall boundaries that marked the three *ahupuaʻa* (land division), Kalawao on the east side, Makanalua in the middle, and Kalaupapa on the west. Those sweet potato patches the archeologists discovered belonged to the ancient people. Other places you can also see small rock enclosures built to shelter sweet potatoes. I learned some of this by reading the letters of Peter Kaeo, Queen Emma's cousin who was confined to Kalawao in the 1870s, and some good historical fiction—*Hawaii* by James Michener and *Molokaʻi* by O.A. Bushnell. I learned even more by talking to some of the real oldtimers who were still alive then, Kenso Seki, Blue Namahoe, Ben Pea, DeCambra and lots of others whose names, I am sad to say, I don't remember now.

But I also led the tours just like how I play music, by ear. I had to know a little history, but the rest came naturally. I was thinking, "What should I do? Tell a little bit about myself? Open up all the way?" I decided to go "all the way." It proved to be a good thing. Soon I was in demand.

The questions the tourists asked helped. I learned right away that the answer I give had better be honest. Many of them had read about Kalauapapa and about leprosy already, and they were looking for confirmation from me. They soon discovered whether I knew what I was talking about. Once in awhile I got a question I couldn't answer, usually about the Protestant or the Mormon Church. I had to say I didn't know. If I lied, they would soon find out.

A lot of the questions had to do with Father Damien, the Catholic priest who served the Settlement from 1873 until his death in 1889. Who was this

Belgian priest who ended up in Hawai'i only because he filled in on a mission when his brother, also a priest, was unable to go?

They wanted to know how Damien got leprosy, years after he had moved to the Settlement. They were interested in his original grave outside St. Philomena's, the church he built, and why his body was exhumed in 1936 and taken to Belgium for reburial in his homeland.

People on the tour wanted to know about the *pali* trail and who built it. They asked about the no children policy, about the hospital and doctors, about why they weren't seeing any residents on their tour.

Sometimes they stumped me, and I'd have to search for answers so I'd be ready the next time. That's how I found out that the Baldwin Home I lived in when I first came to Kalaupapa had originally been the hospital, built in 1932. The complex had included a cottage marked "Condemned" on the map. It was not that the building was condemned, but that the very worst case people stayed there, so disfigured they were hardly recognizable.

When I first heard this when I was a resident at Baldwin Home in the 1940s, I said, "Oh shit, this can't be true." But when I was faced with this question as a tour guide, I looked on a map from when Baldwin Home had been built about 10 or 15 years earlier. There was a little building clearly marked "Condemned Patients Cottage." The map also showed where ladies gave birth in the long building, and where the babies were kept in the nurses' quarters. The parents could only see their babies through a glass window.

On the tour people also asked about me, where I came from, how I got sick, whether there is a cure for Hansen's disease. I followed my idea to go "all the way" and filled them up with everything I knew.

People in my group wanted to know where I went to college. Some thought I was a nurse.

Others guessed I was a teacher. I had to say that I had lipped off to the teacher who tried so hard to get me finish high school.

I especially remember one man who stood beside me near the restrooms when we had stopped for a break. He asked, "Where are all the lepers? I don't see any. Can you show me just one leper person?"

I turned so we were facing each other directly. "Focus on me from head to toe," I said.

"So what are you trying to tell me?"

"You are looking at a patient," I said. "I have been one for many years."

The man was maybe 55 or 60 years old, a bachelor. He might have been Italian, but I could be wrong. He could not or would not believe me. "I want to see people you can tell they have leprosy just by looking at them," he said. "Not like you."

"You're looking for people whose faces are grotesque or are covered with bandages. I'm sorry, there are no more of those. Ever since the sulfone drugs came in use starting in 1946, those people you are looking for are no longer here. They're living, yes, but the drugs have cured or controlled the disease. You will never see those faces you imagine."

"Well, I'll be damned," he said.

The other 19 people on the tour all heard this exchange. They looked surprised.

"I hope today's tour will enlighten you further," I said.

Someone else in the group said, "I think it will."

People always wanted to know about Father Damien contracting leprosy. Consider the elements of his time and place: There was no known medication, let alone a cure. By choice, he was always among the patients, regardless of their condition, dressing their open wounds, bathing them. Often there wasn't even soap. His main concern was the welfare of "his people." When his superiors ordered him to stop, he refused. He kept right on ministering to the living and digging graves for the dead. I could hardly help but develop respect for the man as I learned more and more about what he did at Kalawao in the early decades.

I told them leprosy is a bacterial infection, contagious only after prolonged close contact with someone who has it. It comes in two forms, tuberculoid, which is the least contagious and least serious, and lepromatous, the more serious, the form that used to disfigure people before the sulfone drugs came in after World War II. The bug can live in a person for years before it manifests.

Some say the disease is hereditary, but it's never been proven.

The disease attacks the nerves, the skin and the eyes, often causing loss of eyebrows and other hair, the clawing of fingers and hands, ulcers that take a long time to heal or worsen into bone infections, or sometimes blindness.

Damien worked with patients for more than a decade before he noticed the first symptom—inability to feel when he spilled boiling water on himself. He called the disease by the name of the time: leprosy. Now it's called Hansen's disease after the man who discovered the bacterium that causes it.

Because of answering all those questions, I made a lot of good friends during the tours. I still hear from some who went on my tour many years ago.

My van could seat only 14 people but more would want to sit on the floor just to be on my tour. But the safety rules required each person to be in a seat, and I had to make them go to another van. Eventually Damien Tours bought two buses that each could seat a little more than 20 passengers.

We ran a four-hour tour each weekday. Ike paid $1.75 per hour. Later, when I worked for Damien Tours, Richard paid $2.25. But the wages were on top of tips, which averaged 85 dollars a day, split with the driver.

My reputation grew partly because many of the people who came on the tour arrived via mule down the *pali*. They rode back up in the afternoon. When they dismounted at the stables, they were asked to fill out a question-naire about their experience. They always had something good to say about my abilities as a guide.

But the best thing about this period was that I met the person who created the questionnaire. She also did the public relations, marketing, and booking, and sometimes even served as a mule skinner. In time, we became good friends. We still are. In fact, she is the one who prodded me to write this book, Gena Sasada. Her great-grandfather, a German sugar planter and rancher named Rudolph Meyer, was the Kalaupapa Settlement's first super-intendent, performing his management duties from "topside" at Kalae. Meyer remained in charge throughout Father Damien's years at Kalaupapa (1874-1889) and became good friends with the priest. One of Meyer's granddaughters, Gena's aunt, is a patient here today. Her father, Gene Robins, was the best cowboy we had help us with our cattle drives during my teenage years. Gene Robins' oldest brother, Fred, was the last lighthouse keeper before the Coast Guard automated the facility.

My tour customers loved hearing about those days. I worked for Ike's Scenic Tours for a year or two. Then I worked for a new airline serving Kalaupapa twice a day, Aloha Island Air. My job was to make out tickets, load and unload baggage and cargo, and serve as the "ramp person" who guides the plane to the terminal.

But Aloha Island Air lasted only another few years, and I went to work for Gloria and Richard Marks' Damien Tours.

During these years, about 20 members of the choir at St. John Vianney Catholic Church in Kailua, O'ahu, started coming to Kalaupapa each year. They would come early in the week, offering to clean houses or yards for anyone who wanted their service. They stayed in the Visitors' Quarters. On Thursday evening they gave a formal concert at the altar in St. Francis Catholic Church, which is not far from the Visitors' Quarters. It seemed to me like listening to angels.

Then everyone was invited to join in their meal. Afterward some of us would join them in singing and hula. They brought an electric bass and offered it to me.

"Eh!" I said. "I play only by ear. You folks read music, get all kine instruments. I make one mistake, you going hear um for sure."

Among them they played piccolo, clarinet, violin, guitar and maybe more that I have forgotten. They were glad to have me, and they really didn't care if I made a mistake. We all had so much fun playing all kinds of music that we didn't go home until after midnight.

On the Sabbath the choir would sing at two early Masses at St. Francis, then sing another Mass at the hospital before joining services at Kana'ana Hou Protestant Church and the Mormon Church. Kalaupapa is so small, there are practically no divisions among the Catholics, Protestants and Mormons. That's the way it should be, I think. But I doubt you'd see it very many other places in the world.

During those years of guiding tours and serving with all those organizations I lost most of the rest of my family. When my sister-in-law Nani died, my brother Robert moved to Las Vegas. My daughter moved to California. But then I met another wonderful woman, quite by accident.

One day in 1987 I was driving home in my truck about 5 p.m., after having been along Ho'olehua Beach. I saw a young brunette haole woman walking toward the lighthouse. I did not know who she was, but I offered her a ride even though the weather was fine.

"Aloha," I said. "I'm Henry Nalaielua, one of the residents here. Would you like a ride?"

"Yes. That's very kind of you." She spoke with a French accent. "My name is Cecile," she said.

She was walking back to a cottage in the lighthouse keeper's compound. There hadn't been any Coast Guard personnel there since the 1950s, and some of the facility occasionally was rented by special groups. She was with a group from Belgium that had come to see where Father Damien, the priest from their own country, had done his saintly work, where he had lived and died. The group had just left, but Cecile hoped to stay on to finish some drawings for a children's book about Damien. It was to be like what I would call a comic book series. She hadn't had enough time to complete the field drawings and now she was concerned that she wouldn't be able to stay on for a few more days because she no longer had an official reason to be there.

When we got to the lighthouse complex I asked to see her work. She went in, then came out with a small sketch book and a mid-size drawing book. I knew enough about art to realize her work was excellent.

"I'll help you out," I said. "I'll sponsor you to stay in the Visitors' Quarters."

"Really?"

"Yes," I said. "Sure. Go back in and get your things. I'll take you to the office right now and get you checked in."

The next day I asked her to stay at my house, and she accepted. Soon after that I told Cecile I was an artist too. And that was the beginning of a beautiful friendship that would last many years and lead me to Belgium more than once.

She said she wanted to see the other islands, because Damien had lived on the Big Island in his early years in Hawai'i. So we traveled together to Kona, then around toward Hilo, stopping in Kalapana to see Damien's second painted church. Then we went around the Hāmākua Coast and I showed her the plantation where my father and brothers had worked, and the school I had attended, and the house where I had been born and raised.

Soon a romance developed. Cecile was very pretty, almost as tall as I. I think she was in her late twenties. By this time, I was past 60. I wasn't looking for marriage. In fact, I knew this was temporary, but maybe it could develop into a good relationship.

We traveled more, first on Maui, to Hāna and Waianapanapa, then up to Haleakalā and on to 'Īao Valley. Another day we drove to Waiehu and Kahakuloa, then to Lahaina, and back to Kahului. We toured Moloka'i too, from the west end to Pālā'au Lookout and then to Hālawa Valley and back to Kaunakakai—and Kalaupapa. On Kaua'i we traveled from Hanalei to Kalalau Lookout, staying at a hotel in Lihue.

I watched her draw. She had always been an artist, and had a very interesting technique, not like anything I'd seen locally and not at all like my own. She was very precise, and her drawings were dynamic, alive. I loved watching her work.

After the Kaua'i trip, one of Cecile's friends told her about a convent in Kalihi Valley on O'ahu where she could stay rent-free. After about a week I called her there and asked if I could visit on O'ahu. We arranged to meet at the Bishop Museum gift shop.

When I got there, she was browsing in the book section. I walked to her and kissed her. She held onto me but continued browsing.

"Is there a particular book you're looking for?"

"Yes," she said. "'Kamehameha.'"

"There are many books about Kamehameha," I said.

We looked at a number of them. She chose *Kamehameha the Great* by Stephen Desha.

"Are you sure?" I asked. "You're going to have trouble with all the Hawaiian words."

"That's true," she said. "But it will tell me things I need to know. And as for the Hawaiian words, I have you."

"What if you decide to go home? What then?"

"Okay, I won't buy it," she said. "But help me choose another one."

We settled on *A Young Ali'i* by Mary Kawena Puku'i.

We spent that night at the Blaisdell Hotel downtown on Fort Street, sharing one bed for the first time, slowly introducing each other to the mingling of bodies, embracing, molding together as one. Afterward we went out to supper.

The next day I said, "I could get us a room at the cottage at Leahi Hospital. It wouldn't cost a thing."

"Yes," she said.

Later that same morning, we moved into a room there, on Sunset Avenue in Kaimukī. While Cecile had stayed at the convent she had gone to the beach and had gotten a bad sunburn. We spent the rest of the morning peeling off her skin.

Cecile asked to see a place she had read about, Kūkaniloko out at Wahiawā. I had rented a car, and we drove out to Wahiawā, but I didn't know where the place was, so we asked at a concession stand. Kūkaniloko was the name of an ancient chief, and the place was where royal women gave birth, maybe as far back as the thirteenth century. It's thought of as "the birthing stone" but there were many stones there, not like our one rock at Kalaupapa. I thought this place must be visited quite often, to judge from the number of ti leaf offerings laid on the stones.

Cecile took pictures with her Nikon, adding them to her collection of photos of all the historical places we had visited. She said she hoped to somehow use this special place in her book.

We stayed at the cottage about a week. All told, we had been together three or four weeks. Cecile had been in Hawai'i almost four months. She decided it was time to leave.

"I have to go home," she said. "But will you come to Belgium to see me?"

"I don't know. It's so far away."

"Please think about it."

"I will. I'll write to you."

I had paid for everything we did together. A couple of days before she left, she said, "How much money do I owe you?"

"None," I said. "It doesn't matter. This has all been totally worth my time and money."

"No," she said. "I insist."

She went to the bank, made a withdrawal, and paid me the amount she thought she should. It seemed to me she paid me back every penny.

I took her to the airport. We got a skycap to take her luggage, and we went to sit at her gate. We sat a few minutes and then I got up.

"I'll be back," I said. "Stay here."

I returned with two carnation lei, one pink, one red. I put them both around her neck and we kissed for a long time. She waited as long as she could to board. Then she kissed me one last time and walked onto the jetway.

I stayed there until the plane rolled out and took off, thinking of how I missed Cecile already. I drove back to Leahi and stayed the night, and the next day I flew to Kalaupapa. I was alone again.

I got my janitor job at the hospital back easily because no one had taken it all the time I had been gone. Ike's Tours had really failed as a business even before I left, so it wasn't a possibility. But I went to work for Damien Tours instead.

Cecile and I wrote letters, and occasionally I called long distance.

Peter Thompson replaced Henry Law as park superintendent in 1988. During his time, the Park Service did major renovation of our little airport. It included a complete overhaul and extension of the runway, improvement of the terminal, new blacktop for all the paved roads and parking areas.

The construction crew came upon many modern artifacts such as broken china, buttons and modern fishhooks, all of which were gathered and catalogued by the Park archeologist. They also discovered the site of a huge ancient sweet potato patch at the west end of the runway and burial sites—although not human remains—throughout the airport area. The archeologist made a report, and so did I, as a member of the Moloka'i Burial Council. Although the burials were not too far from the end of Papaloa Cemetery that runs between the road and the long beach—the cemetery that was so damaged in the 1946 tidal wave—they were from a time that predated Kalaupapa Settlement.

The only one in which we actually found remains was the sandy grave of a child about six months old. A stone had been placed on this baby's head, one indication that it had been buried prior to 1865. The head was not crushed, but rather placed carefully, to keep dogs away. My job, as a member of the Burial Council, was to see that this baby had a proper burial.

We made a coconut-leaf basket to hold the little bones and then, with a prayer, we put the basket in a cement box and buried the baby at the bottom of the flagpole at the airport.

Through all this, I thought about Cecile. Finally I decided I would make a trip to Belgium.

It was January 1988. I got my picture taken at topside Moloka'i for my passport and went to Honolulu to get my actual passport. I still had some warm clothes from when I was in Carville, so that was good.

Just before I left, I stopped at an airport lei stand and bought carnation lei for Cecile's parents and a double *maile* lei for her. I also purchased four loaves of Portuguese sweet bread from Honolulu's famous Leonard's Bakery and two cans of macadamia nuts for gifts.

This was a far longer trip than any I had been on—Honolulu to Los Angeles, then to Chicago, New York, London and finally Brussels, at least 36 hours from first takeoff to final touchdown. I was able to sleep a lot of the time, so when we landed in Brussels, I really felt fine.

I walked into the terminal and there was Cecile waiting on the balcony, smiling. I climbed up the stairs to her, took out the *maile* lei, draped it on her shoulders, and kissed her.

When we picked up my baggage from customs, the box I had packed with the bread and macadamia nuts was open. One of the officials said, "Somebody's going to be lucky with these presents from Hawai'i."

"Yes!" Cecile smiled. "Me! I'm the lucky one!"

At the terminal we boarded an electric train for a short ride to where her mother would pick us up. It was about 5:30 in the afternoon and it was cold. We went to Cecile's mother's home, where I met Cecile's father.

"Welcome," he said. "Sorry about this weather. Cecile tells us it's always warm and sunny in Hawai'i."

Surprisingly, after such a long trip, the two carnation lei looked good. I gave Cecile's mother one of them and kissed her cheek. She had never received a lei before, or even seen one. The second lei I gave to Cecile and told her to put it around her father's neck and give him a kiss. All during supper both her parents wore their lei and kept smelling them from time to time. They really enjoyed the sweet bread, and ate all the macadamia nuts with their wine.

About 10:30 p.m. Cecile's father drove us to her place about a mile away. She had a large third-floor apartment, three bedrooms, a huge parlor, kitchen and bath. The trip had caught up with me and now I was very tired, so we retired for the night.

The next day we went back to her parents' home and her father took me on a tour that included the college where he taught math. We also went to Waterloo, where Napoleon lost his famous battle. We visited so many places I couldn't remember their names. We went by the palace where the king resides, a huge building covering more than a block. I remember the open-air markets, under tents. One thing about these markets in the middle of winter—no flies!

Later I rented a car of my own, so Cecile and I could drive out of Brussels. Before we set off, we went back to her apartment to get warm clothing, because the weather can be very changeable.

We took the autobahn, Europe's version of a freeway, five lanes without any speed limit!

Our first stop, about an hour away, was the village of Tremeloo, where Father Damien had grown up, the youngest son and seventh child of the eight children born to Frans and Ann-Catherine DeVeuster. His name was Joseph.

The village looked like any little village. The little church Damien had attended was even smaller than St. Philomena's at Kalawao. Cecile pointed out Damien's family home, and places he had visited. After an hour or so, we drove on to Louvain, the little town nearby. Now all of Louvain is Damien. In 1936 the King of Belgium requested that Damien's body be exhumed from its resting place at Kalawao. It was reburied in Louvain. Two years later, the Catholic Church began proceedings for Damien's beatification, which finally happened in 1995.

The tomb was in a crypt at St. Joseph's Church, inside and down some stairs. It was plain, nothing around it, not even flowers. Nobody but us was there. It all made me sad. At Kalawao he had been buried outside in the open air, and from time to time people would place fresh flowers his grave. I thought about his life on Moloka'i more than 100 years ago, and thought about him being reburied here. He was close to Hawai'i, and to this place too. It had been about 50 years since I first had read of Damien and thought to myself, "Wow." Now I really felt his presence moving inside me. No wonder the expression "moving" means "stirring strong feelings or emotions." This was the "big wow."

We drove to the DeVeuster family farm out in the country, but there wasn't really much left to see.

We returned to Cecile's apartment for the night. Then she took me touring to other sights. We stopped at a castle that was complete with a moat and stone staircases too narrow for more than one person. I imagined the fights that would have taken place on those stairs. At the top of the castle were square holes in the stone walls, from which archers fired on their attackers.

Beneath the castle were torture chambers. The items on display included a guillotine, with a heavy blade honed to its thinnest point. There was the infamous "rack," a torture table to stretch a human body to an unimaginable length. Then there was the water torture table. And a place for finger torture.

At the end of two weeks, it was time for me to return to Hawai'i. My 12 days with Cecile and her parents were great. Now it was "aloha 'oe." I did not know that I would return to Damien's land and see Cecile again in the near future.

*****

When I returned home, I involved myself in the OHA Kupuna Program again. Through it, and thanks to our teacher, Malcolm Naea Chun, I learned a lot. As a Hawaiian, I learned about other native cultures, especially the Maori of Aotearoa (New Zealand) and the Pueblo Indians. Through the program, we visited both.

The program started at the East-West Center at the University of Hawai'i, where I met Walter Desheno, a Pueblo Indian from New Mexico, and another Indian with him, Narajano. Soon we visited New Mexico, and I stayed a week with Desheno, sightseeing and learning. We visited a place of caves where the early Indians lived. It was like a maze—you come out somewhere else! And talk about mean air-conditioning!

We talked a lot about how different the Indian and Hawaiian cultures are, but we found in some things we were the same. They have a place like a *hālau*—a meeting place. And they have a taboo on some things, like taking pictures. We went to a particular party where a tourist tried to take pictures. Those Indians whacked the camera right out of the guy's hands!

The Maori were more like Hawaiians. OHA's purpose in all this was to share cultures. But OHA didn't pay for the trips. We did. Yet I remain most appreciative of being able to visit the Maori and the Pueblo people. This type of cultural exchange is something the world should practice. It fosters learning from and about one another. Both those experiences will live within me the rest of my life.

Also through OHA, I traveled to the various islands of Hawai'i to speak to both *kupuna* (elders) and school children about what it's like to have the dreaded Hansen's disease.

I especially remember one young boy in a class. It was at Nānākuli or Benjamin Parker Elementary. At the end of my talk, he raised his hand.

"Do fingers really fall right off your hand?" he asked.

"Where did you hear this?" I asked gently.

"A boy told me."

"Well," I said. "Now you know that I am a person with Hansen's disease. I can tell you for sure that fingers don't fall off your hands." I held out my hands. "See? I have all my fingers. They are kind of crabbed up so the fingers won't straighten out. But I have had this disease since I was just as old as you. Now I am an old man and I still have all my fingers." I turned my hands over a couple of times so all the kids could see.

"Now," I said. "It could sometimes happen that a person might get such a serious infection in a finger that it just can't heal. But even then, the finger wouldn't just fall off. It would just kind of shrink back. But it would still be there."

The kid's big mouth was wide open but he didn't say another word. As I was leaving, the teacher said, "Too bad he's too young to understand."

"I don't think that's true," I replied. "It was a very personal question. For some reason, he had to know the answer."

She looked at me thoughtfully.

"You know," I continued, "The subject of Hansen's disease is shocking and scary and horrifying. I talk about it, standing before students as a patient they can actually see. Even though these students are young, I bet they will remember at least some of what I said for a long time to come."

In addition to the educational programs about Hansen's disease, I also got involved with the Hawaiian Language Immersion Program, Pūnana Leo. I was especially glad to be part of a program aimed at saving the Hawaiian language, which was taken away from our people when Hawai'i became part of the U.S. when my parents were young. I really think that it would be proper for Hawaiian language study to be mandatory in all schools, since this is our mother tongue and the first language of these islands.

The only thing was, the Pūnana Leo people who asked me to be a language consultant thought I was an expert. But the last time I really spoke Hawaiian was in 1936 with my grandmother. I can speak, but I have to think hard. It's two words at a time—and don't rush me. Once many years earlier at Kalaupapa I was working as a carpenter and I heard two of the staff workmen speaking in Hawaiian. I said something to them in Hawaiian and they looked at me like a miracle had happened. After that I tried learning to write in Hawaiian, just picking it up as best I could. I was lucky to have the instinct for it, to be able to write, and speak some. But all this hardly turned me into an expert. Still, I was of some use to Pūnana Leo, and glad to help.

In June of 1988 I went to Europe again, this time because I was invited as part of a group from Kalaupapa to participate in the Thirteenth International Leprosy Congress to be held in The Hague in Holland. The Congress only happened once in about five years, so it was quite special. American doctors included some from Carville, of course, and then there were representatives from all over the world, from nations like Kenya, Ethiopia, India, China and Japan. Our Kalaupapa group of about ten included patients Bill and Elroy Malo, Bernard Punikaia and Gloria Marks and the National Park Superintendent Henry Law and his wife, Anwei Skinses Law. Stephanie Castillo from the *Honolulu Star-Bulletin* and a photographer from Kaneʻohe, Bill Ballback, were there too. Our Kalaupapa group really stood out because we sang songs of the islands. We didn't perform on a schedule, just picked up and went anywhere. It was just "hang loose." I had my ʻukulele, and everyone sang Hawaiian songs.

It turned out that this was the first such conference to include patients. I discovered my attitude about leprosy was not shared by everyone attending, especially, it seemed, people from Africa. If they could get away without admitting to being patients, they would.

I met a patient whose behavior made me ask, "Are you trying to hide something?"

"I'm not trying to hide. I'm just playing it safe."

"What are you hiding from, in a leprosy conference?" I asked. "Half the people here are patients. I say, show that you are what you are. So you have leprosy. So what? You're the same person regardless. I can't see myself lying. Or hiding. I have Hansen's disease, or leprosy, whatever you want to call it. It's not my fault."

My little speech was only to that one person. But Bernard and Bill Malo, representing all of us patients in addressing the whole assembly about our experiences with Hansen's disease, pretty well said the same thing. They were well received, and many people asked them for copies of their talks.

After the week of meetings, the whole Kalaupapa group took the train to Brussels. Considering how we were seated on the train, I thought it was a miracle that we didn't lose a single bag. A number of people from Louvain came to meet us at the station. They drove us to a monastery of the Brothers of the Sacred Hearts, where we would stay during our time in Louvain. The Order of the Sacred Hearts of Jesus and Mary is the order to which Father Damien belonged. The people all received us with warm and friendly greetings. Even a Brother who had lived at Baldwin Home at Kalaupapa came to see us. One of the Fathers guided us around the monastery.

Cecile joined us, staying with us in the monastery for two nights.

By bus we visited all the places Damien had lived, and also a museum in Tremeloo that displayed Damien memorabilia, things like his bed, and his chasuble and other vestments. I remember the room being so plain, with nothing for furniture but his bed and a chiffonier, without even a mirror.

Our last stop was to visit Damien's tomb, in the crypt beneath the church in Louvain. The crypt was maybe 18 by 40 feet, with a solid granite sarcophagus in the center.

We had not planned a thing. But we recited the Lord's Prayer in unison, in English. And then Anwei Law said spontaneously, "I want you to sing 'Hawai'i Aloha.'"

So we sang, standing in a circle holding hands. Makia Malo did a solo. The crypt had a nice resonance to it, with the sound of our a cappella harmony hanging in the confined air. Then Anwei said, "And maybe 'Aloha 'Oe.' You sing it. We cannot."

So we sang our farewell to Damien. What a warm and giving memorial it was just to be at his tomb.

At the end of our time in Louvain, Cecile came with us as we boarded a train for France.

Cecile helped us communicate with the gendarmes when we crossed the border. As they inspected our identification, Cecile told them we were from Hawai'i. They were surprised.

When we arrived in Paris we took a bus to our hotel. In the evening, we went separate ways. Cecile and I went to look for a place to eat, then went for a walk on the Champs Elysées. When it got dark we returned to the hotel for a night of much needed rest.

The next day we had planned some sightseeing but there weren't enough cabs at the hotel for all of us, so Cecile and I walked once again, to the Arc de Triomphe. The streets were the widest I had ever seen. Not only were there lots of cars, but buses as well—and then there were trains traveling underground that I mistook for streetcars! We had breakfast at a café, then took the Metro underground and came out on the Seine. The river seemed awfully wide to me.

We took a boat ride. Two kids—a boy and a girl about 10 and 12—seated themselves on either side of me. They hung onto me and said, "Papa!" Then I felt their hands in my pockets.

I thought if they picked my pocket, I'd throw them in the river. But I just grabbed them by the hands, gently. They were just kids.

After that, we walked several blocks to the Cathedral de Notre Dame. It is the most immense church I've ever seen, with so many majestic stained windows. And good grief—the gargoyles! I stood outside looking up, and the first thing coming to mind was the Hunchback of Notre Dame.

At the entry Cecile pointed to a sign. "See that, Henry?"

I looked. The sign said, in both French and English, "Watch Your Wallet." Then she pointed at the wallet in my hand. "Put that away."

A church always has an altar, but inside there was altar after altar. And it seemed to be a church inside a church, with the 12 apostles looking down on us. Somehow four Masses were all going at once.

We also saw the Eiffel Tower, which left me in awe as I contemplated how it was built. When we got there, it was raining, so we didn't go up, but instead went to the Museum of Arts. Cecile had not been there before. It was another huge building, eight floors, I think. We went through one floor and that was enough for me. There is just so much, you don't know where to go. When we returned to the hotel we took a short nap.

We spent our last night together. In the morning, she came with me to the airport.

"I think this is it," I said. I hate good-byes.

"I guess so." Cecile looked at me, smiling a little.

There was no sense lingering. We kissed good-bye, and that was it. I would never see Cecile again. Of course, I had thought that the last time I had left her, six months earlier in Belgium.

It had been a wonderful trip but I was glad to be on my way home. It was summer of 1988. I did not expect to see Europe again.

*****

During all this time I was still on the Patient Council and the Burial Council. Then, in the early nineties, when the Native Hawaiian Health Care Systems were funded by the U.S. Congress, another duty came my way.

The system on Moloka'i was named Na Pu'uwai and was under the leadership of Dr. Emmett Aluli, who is now medical director of Moloka'i General Hospital, and social worker Billy Akutagawa, who now heads Na Pu'uwai. I worked with them on the Burial Council. They brought a small group to Kalaupapa to recruit a board member for Na Pu'uwai.

The patients all basically said, "Nobody like do this. We no like go topside. Na Pu'uwai no can help us." I agreed, but not completely and so I told Dr. Aluli and Billy I would serve. Now Na Pu'uwai is a thriving health care center serving Moloka'i and Lana'i. I'm still on the Board although, like the Board of Health, I have not been able to attend meetings recently.

For awhile I didn't see the hidden benefit—a growing friendship with both Emmett and Billy as time went on. Every time I flew topside to attend a meeting, Billy picked me up at the airport. Many times I stayed overnight with Emmett at his place in Ho'olehua. I'd have my own bedroom upstairs. Sometimes I'd rather sleep on the porch, where it was cool and I could see the stars. He was an excellent chef and he'd cook for me and whoever else he had staying with him. And we'd talk about all kinds of things, including Hokūle'a, the famous sailing canoe, and Kaho'olawe, the small island in the lee of Maui that was a major political issue and with which Emmett had been involved since the early 1970s. He really is an oldtime Hawaiian doctor, completely friendly, very warm, helping a lot of people. They go for medicine, he doesn't charge.

About 1992, when the airport project was finished, Peter Thompson moved from the Settlement to topside Moloka'i where his wife lived, and from there supervised the repair of the *pali* trail. The trail was in such bad condition from the ravages of the weather that it actually had to be closed for about three years while the repairs were made. It meant that the Moloka'i Mule Ride, which had brought visitors on guided tours to Kalaupapa since 1974, stopped in 1992. But the trail—and the mule ride—reopened in 1995, and now a number of Park Service and Department of Health employees "commute" to work from topside Moloka'i by hiking down and up the trail each day. And the mule ride brings visitors once again.

When the trail was back in service, Thompson retired and a promising young man named Dean Alexander came to us as superintendent. His interests ran more to studies in Hawaiian history. He invited a Hawaiian language study group from O'ahu to come to do research on ancient *heiau* and other places on the peninsula used by ancient Hawaiians. These included *ko'a*, fishing shrines that also served as landmarks for fishing grounds in the ocean. The studies documented a canoe slide where ancient residents launched their fishing expeditions, and a *hōlua* (sled) slide on the slopes of Kauhakō Crater.

Alexander cleared two *heiau* near the road to Kalawao of impassable thickets of Christmas berry brush. The one nearest the road was—and still is—in especially poor repair from animals climbing on it to forage. No one knows the names of the *heiau* or their ancient purposes.

Alexander —fortyish, tall, with brown hair and green eyes—also joined the *hālau* hula (hula school) at the Settlement, under *kumu* (teacher) Pauline Meheula, one of our nurses. He danced without being stiff, just as if he belonged. And, amazingly, he learned to *kāhea*—do the stanza calls in a danced chant—just as smooth as silk. I never did see him at the bar, though, or even fishing.

In 1993 he sponsored a program to bring people together to discuss how we could educate the world about Hansen's disease, with the idea of helping those struggling under the stigma of the terms "leper" or "leprosy."

About 15 visitors from the mainland, Japan and other parts of the world joined us for three days, staying at the Visitors' Quarters. The first day we took our guests on a comprehensive tour, with me giving the history/patient part and Dean doing the part about the Park Service. The next day's discussions started with the strong feeling from Carville that "leprosy" must be replaced with "Hansen's disease." But it's not that simple. If I say "Hansen's disease," I have to explain it. If I say "leprosy," it scares everybody, and they jump to conclusions. It's a problem either way.

The third day we threw a lū'au for all these guests. It wasn't quite like the old Baldwin Home lū'au, but close. Kalaupapa's *hālau* danced, including Dean Alexander. David Kupele, my friend from long ago, was our musician and singer, coming from Honolulu where he lived. Bernard Punikaia and I joined in, with bass and 'ukulele, and of course, our voices. I remember singing "Sunset at Kalaupapa," the words of which had been composed by a former patient, Samson Kuahine, and which had been set to music and recorded by the famous Harry Owens. With the money he made from royalties, Samson had bought the Settlement a baby grand piano.

The whole session seemed to have a big and energizing impact on the participants, especially about the need to educate the public about Hansen's disease, and how important it is to call it that rather than the old Biblical name.

The next year, as a member of the Patient Advisory Council I was invited to participate in a gathering of some 20 people from various National Historical Parks around the U.S. Mike McCarten, the Department of Health Administrator for Kalaupapa Settlement, and I were guests of Dean Alexander for a week of meetings at the Presidio in San Francisco. It turned out that Mike and I were the only people there who were not part of the National Park System. Dean's purpose in bringing Mike and me to these meetings was to have some input from the point of view of Department of Health Administration and the Patients' Advisory Council. I learned at least as much as I shared, as I listened to others describe ways of getting the most out of meager budgets for these small parks.

Although we toured a number of parks in the area, including the Presidio itself, for me the highlight was going by boat Alcatraz Island. It had been first fortified by the Spanish, then became a U.S. military prison in 1859. In 1933 the U.S. converted it to a federal maximum security penitentiary that came to be called "The Rock." By the time I visited, Alcatraz had been part of the Golden Gate National Recreation Area for about 20 years.

Our group was part of a regular tour with a ranger. "The Rock" itself was a little like Kalaupapa, surrounded by water, except that we have cliffs on one side. But the facility, where a whole group of gangsters, the Big Boys, lived out their lives, was nothing like Kalaupapa's little jail.

The next year, Dean Alexander left Kalaupapa for a better job in a bigger park. I guess it's a good thing for these guys to move on. They might get stale. But I thought of all he'd done to document more of Kalaupapa's history, and about the big Hansen's disease meeting. I thought about the Presidio, and about him dancing with our hula *hālau*, and I remembered that he was a man who talked very little, but he really listened. There were no farewell parties or speeches, but lots of people came to the airport to say good-bye, including me. He was my friend.

*****

In Hawai'i there was a renewed move afoot to have Damien beatified. In the Catholic system, beatification is the last step in the long canonization process by which someone becomes a saint. It involves much study of the person's life and ministry, and requires a miracle shown to have occurred by the person's intercession. The miracle must have happened after his death. It seemed awfully complicated.

I put my efforts into something smaller, joining with other patients to petition the Catholic Church to return Damien to Hawai'i, specifically to Kalaupapa. Of course we wanted his whole remains to return, but in the end we were happy to have a small relic.

Finally beatification was approved, and in 1994 I became part of a group from Hawai'i that attended the ceremonies in Damien's hometown of Tremeloo in Belgium. Shortly before the date set, Pope John Paul II broke his hip and postponed the Mass. It was too late to cancel our plans, though, so we went and had a Mass anyway, without the Pope.

The Vatican rescheduled for a year later, but in Brussels rather than Tremeloo. So in 1995 we went back. Our Hawai'i delegation, more than 100 of us, stayed at a swank hotel in Brussels for several days, visiting various places and churches. St. John Vianney's choir, our dear friends from Kailua, O'ahu, sang in some of the churches. We toured a whole day, even going to the church where Damien had been baptized.

The Pope's Mass was held June 4 at Koelkelberg Basilica. It was a huge cathedral, but the Mass was to be held outside. We were bussed from the hotel. I looked outside and thought, "Looks like maybe rain. I going stay inside the bus." I sat there.

Somebody said, "Come!"

And I did.

Thousands of people had gathered. Our contingent was not seated together. My seat was perhaps 75 yards from the front, and I could see the Pope clearly.

As soon as things began, it started raining. And not just raining, but pouring, for the whole hour of the ceremony. Only a few people had umbrellas. The Pope was under a canopy. Me, I just got wet. Everyone else got soaked too. About 40 lay priests came around to give everyone Communion.

Then the Pope blessed Damien's relic and presented it to the representative we patients had selected, Meli Pili, and Randy King, who had arranged our entire trip. The relic is the remains of Damien's right hand. His body had been exhumed again in the 1950s for the Catholic Church's forensic study that is part of beatification proceedings. They didn't know then it would take another four decades to complete the process. When the examinations were finished, Damien's bones were separated and put in individual marked boxes made of zinc. When it came time to remove his right hand for us, the Church opened the sarcophagus again, and brought out the correct box. The whole idea of relics is foreign to Americans, but to Europeans it's quite natural, kind of like having a lock of someone's hair as a physical connection to the person.

At the end of the Mass, the Pope's attendants tried to get him to leave. He said, "No, not until I see the hula."

The dance was performed—in the rain—by Hālau Hula o Ma'iki.

The next morning a Mass was held in our hotel at 6:15 a.m. especially for us from Kalaupapa to receive the blessing of Damien's relic and kiss the box in which it lay. Plenty people came.

The reliquary, the beautiful koa box made by the famous 'ukulele maker Sam Kamaka, was on an altar, ringed with ti leaves. A prayer was chanted in Hawaiian, and the *hālau* danced again. Father Joseph Bukoski, who headed the Damien Commission in Hawai'i, and some other priests broke the wax seal on the reliquary. He pulled out the zinc box and gave it to Pua VanDorpe, the *kapa* (barkcloth) master from the Big Island. She wrapped it in ceremonial *kapa* she had made. First she wrapped the paper-thin white layer with a border design that included two hearts and a cross. The outer, sturdier *kapa* was black, signifying high rank.

After communion, Bukoski carried the bundle to our Kalaupapa group, and we kissed it. My feeling then is not easy to describe. Emotional. Eerie. Something that stirred me. I wasn't thinking about touching heaven. Touching Damien was enough.

When all the ceremonies were over some of our group stayed on to travel more.

But I was in the group that came home with Damien's relic. When we got off the plane in Honolulu it was evening. The relic went immediately to the Cathedral of Our Lady of Peace downtown on Fort Street. From there it spent the next few weeks touring the islands.

Then, on July 15 the Church arranged a huge public reception in Honolulu at 'Iolani Palace. Cardinal Godfried Daneels of Belgium was a special guest. I was on the program as a speaker too. I have no idea how I was chosen. I think someone said, "Oh, go ask Henry for say something." I prepared some notes and stuck the paper in the pocket of my aloha shirt, under the ginger lei someone had given me. But when it came time to speak, I just couldn't talk looking at a piece of paper.

I stood up at the lectern. I thought about the first time I saw Damien's grave in Louvain, and about the beatification only last month in Brussels. It all took just an instant. My feeling of dedication to the man was so strong, I knew I was going to say the right thing. A complete calm came over me. I left the notes in my pocket and spoke from my heart.

"Damien spent months coming across the world's oceans just to serve in a small place like Kalaupapa," I began. "He came, he saw, he conquered."

I didn't have a chance to finish. I heard the scraping of folding chairs arranged on the paving in front of the Palace steps. People were getting up. Finally, much to my amazement, I realized they were giving me a standing ovation.

A week later, the Bishop of Honolulu, Francis X. DiLorenzo, came to Kalaupapa to preside at an open-air Mass, and this time we buried the relic in its beautiful reliquary in Damien's original grave outside St. Philomena's tiny country church. Four patients assisted in pounding the dowels to secure the reliquary lid—Bernard Punikaia, Nelly McCarty, Richard Marks and Kenso Seki. When the reliquary was lowered into its resting place and the concrete slab replaced, many of the 500 people who had come to attend this Mass heaped the grave with lei and bouquets.

This time there was no rain. It was a bright, shiny day, with the tradewinds welcoming Father Damien home. He will not leave again. This was Damien's true home. And it is mine. Kalaupapa, the home of my heart.

Epilogue

Honolulu 2006

I met Henry just about the time of Damien's beatification, when he helped me with my assignments to write articles about Kalaupapa. By the time I saw him again, five years had passed. In that interim, his mule ride friend, Gena Sasada, moved from topside Moloka'i to the Settlement in 1995 and became manager of the Kalaupapa Store.

She knew she had one good friend at the Settlement—Henry. They had actually met years earlier when her kid brother and Henry played music together. When she worked for the Moloka'i Mule Ride in the eighties, that cinched her friendship with Henry. Whenever a muleskinner got sick, Gena had to fill in. One of the first times she came down the trail, there was Henry, waiting for his party. She dismounted and hugged him.

"So are you going on my tour?" he asked.

"No. Why?"

"Well, if you're going to run the mule ride, maybe it would help to learn something about Kalaupapa and what I do on the tour."

So she went. And she found out why tourists filled in her questionnaire with compliments for Henry. He shared himself and his knowledge, and he sought even more knowledge from others, such as an archeologist who came with the Park Service. They all shared what they knew and he in turn shared it on his tours.

After she moved to Kalaupapa, sometimes Gena and Henry drove around the peninsula in his red pickup, out to Kalawao, or to Hoʻolehua Beach near the lighthouse. Invariably, as they passed something they'd both seen countless times, he'd say something like, "You know that pantry at the staff quarters? That used to be a post office."

His well of such historical details never seemed to run dry, and neither did his willingness to share his experiences as a patient. In hundreds of hours talking with Henry, Gena, 17 years his junior, came to regard him not only as a dear friend, but as a teacher and mentor. She wrote down his teachings as they came in bits and pieces, and uses them all as she takes friends around Kalaupapa.

For about five months in 1998, when Gena had been at Kalaupapa about four years, a Belgian film company did the location work on the Kalaupapa peninsula for a movie called *Molokaʻi, The Story of Father Damien*. Kris Kristofferson played the Settlement superintendent, Rudolph Meyer, Gena's great-grandfather. The filming was done at Kalawao, on the east side of the peninsula near Damien's little church, St. Philomena's. But that's all that is left of the original Settlement, and the movie company had to create sets to approximate the homes and other buildings of the 1880s. Henry and almost all the other patients appeared in the movie as extras.

About the same time, Henry and Gena made a trip to the Big Island and he showed her Nīnole, the little plantation town where he had spent his first ten years. He had once described its size to me as "having a post office as big as a two-hole outhouse." The new post office is somewhat larger and sugarcane is no longer a viable crop. But he showed her the cane field where his father and brothers took care of the flumes, and the old gas station, and even the house where he was born and lived his first ten years.

Not long after that trip, when Gena and Henry were sitting in her house "talking story" one day, it came to her that Henry should write down all that had happened in his life.

"For what?" he asked.

"Only two patients have done it, the last in 1988. Besides, it's your legacy."

He laughed.

"No," she insisted. "You should write it. You might be the last patient able to do it."

"Nah," he said. "For what?"

"For plenty," she said, starting to sound desperately eloquent. Like Henry, she can speak the King's English or pidgin, and often mingles them. "You don't write this down, it going be lost. Too much of it is just in your head. Your story is part of our story, and our heritage that we should pass on to our grandchildren and their children. Someday there will be none of you left, and that will be the end of an era that is an important part of Hawai'i's history."

He still balked. She still badgered. The two hardheads kept it up, until one day Henry said, "OK. Tell me what to do."

She took a flying guess. "Write down something about something and I'll go type it up."

By the time she had typed up three of his writings, Gena decided they didn't know what they were doing. She had seen one of my Kalaupapa articles, and another piece on an unrelated topic in another magazine, *Island Scene*. She couldn't remember where the Kalaupapa piece had been published. But she finally hunted up a copy of *Island Scene* and found an e-mail address for the editor, Bill Harby. She wrote to him, explaining that she wanted to get in touch with me for some advice about how to proceed with Henry's story.

At the time, I didn't have e-mail. But Bill is a sweetheart, and so he printed out Gena's message and mailed it to me with an actual stamp.

I called her on the phone immediately. It was a Sunday.

A couple of weeks had passed since she had begun her search for me and she had almost given up hope that I would answer. She explained her mission. It may have taken her three minutes. In that short time, listening to her completely open tone as well as to her words, I could tell that she was my spirit sister. She felt it too. It was as though we'd known each other forever.

"Sure, I'll help you," I said, in the same words Henry had used when I had been the one asking for aid. "Let me see what you have done so far, and I'll make some suggestions."

Later she went over to Henry's house to tell him how she had made this amazing search for me and that I had agreed to help them. When she got near the end of her search story, he said, "Why you do that? I get her phone number!"

The two hardheads laughed and laughed.

I looked over the pages of the story they sent, suggested they keep on in the same vein, and volunteered to help shape the various pieces into a whole. That was late 1999.

I live in Oregon. I planned to come to Kalaupapa in April, and we would work together for a few concentrated days.

About the time I got to Oʻahu, Henry landed in a Honolulu hospital. My husband and I went to visit. I went to visit again. Henry was able to converse, but was not up to working on his story. His foot ulcer was acting up again, big time.

I decided to go ahead with the plan to fly to Kalaupapa. My husband and I spent the four days with Gena.

Of course I had never met her, but there she was, waiting for us at the little airport. I grew up in a huge Hawaiian family full of aunties and uncles and hugs and kisses, but never have I seen a warmer, more welcoming smile. It was true, she was my spirit sister.

Henry's foot problem was so bad he was on Oʻahu for weeks after surgery on the bone. Eventually he went home and the next year I finally got to visit him at Kalaupapa. He was driving all right but walking on crutches. He'd written many more pages of his story by hand, Gena had typed them, and we reviewed them. I'm sure he grew quite weary of me asking question after question, to fill in the blank spots where he had either forgotten some details or thought they weren't interesting.

One day at Kalaupapa, to break the question sessions, Henry, Gena and I rode in his truck out to Papaloa Cemetery. The graves of his sisters had washed away with the 1946 tidal wave, but he thought he could find the stone for his Uncle Joseph.

We had to walk back and forth some, Henry's crutches unstable in the sand under the beach grass covering the dunes where the cemetery had been laid out.

At last we saw the marker, flat cement with a cross in horizontal relief and two empty receptacles for flowers. The name had been carved by hand and, after some 80 years, was hard to read. Finally we made it out: Joe Palau Nalaielua. Born Feb. 1, 1904. Died Dec. 5, 1913.

Until he stumbled on this grave in the 1960s, Henry had not known that his uncle Joe had ever lived.

Henry had had 30 years to think about it. He had told me the story of his discovery back in 1995, but now that I saw the gravestone, I had to think about Joe for quite awhile. I thought about Henry's sisters too.

The Kalaupapa files include a picture of Evelyn taken the day she was admitted to Kalihi Hospital, November 16, 1927. She was 16. Her hair is cut short, in the fashion of the twenties, and she holds her right hand over the center of her chest. She looks worried, sad, scared, as if she knows she is betrayed by a disease that will end her earthly years before long. Indeed, she was transferred to Kalaupapa in less than two years and died there in November 1935. She'd been married two and-a-half years. She was 24.

The files don't even show a picture of little Christina. She just appears as a typed record, entering Kalaupapa in January of 1933, when she was nine, and dying there in October 1935, a month before her sister.

Each time I returned to Oregon, Henry wrote more of his recollections. Gena typed them into her computer and forwarded them to me, and the three of us developed a system that worked pretty well.

We hit a few more health hitches in the process. Once Henry got a nasty case of pneumonia that had to be treated in Honolulu in the hospital. Another time he was airlifted to Honolulu in diabetic shock.

After all this, the doctors insisted that he stay in the little Kalaupapa hospital at night—and he insisted that he drive over to his house during the day. By this time, Henry was on crutches part of the time, and in a wheelchair while in the hospital.

In the good spells between health episodes, we worked on his story. And he continued to draw and paint.

By late 2002 Henry was residing most of the time at Hale Mohalu, the Hansen's disease unit of Honolulu's Leahi Hospital that had replaced the old Hale Mohalu in Pearl City. Diabetes had taken such a toll that, after much persuasion by his doctors, he opted for kidney dialysis three times a week, a service that was not available at Kalaupapa.

He was still reluctant about dialysis, but after a few sessions, he felt much better. It was worth it to spend so much time "on the machine." When next I saw him, working with him for a few weeks at Hale Mohalu, he could leave his wheelchair only to get in and out of a car and other such moves but he was much more energetic.

During that time, in early 2003, he had his first one-man art show, a display of 28 of his drawings and paintings at Native Books in Honolulu. Many of the selected works, including the large oil he painted for his old Carville friend Louis Boudreaux, were Kalaupapa scenes. Some pencil drawings depicted ancient Hawaiians, one a vintage gas pump in his home village of Nīnole. One small work titled *Red Blanket* was a painting of a nude woman.

Wryly funny as ever, when someone asked him at the opening reception about *Red Blanket*, Henry smiled and said, "No comment."

The dialysis regimen three times a week meant that Henry really could only fly to Kalaupapa for an occasional weekend visit. Hale Mohalu's hospital rooms and parade of nurses came to resemble more and more a jail and jailers.

Henry began what turned out to be a year-long effort to get a dialysis machine at Kalaupapa, to benefit other patients as well as himself. His old friends Emmett Aluli and Billy Akutagawa were among the many who helped make this happen.

Henry returned to Kalaupapa in April of 2004. Home! Again! He was happy, even though the medical staff required that he live in the little hospital there.

But within a couple of months his heart started acting up, to a degree that once again required him to reside at Hale Mohalu, close to the most extensive medical facilities.

So, by summer of 2004 there he was, back in jail, continuing dialysis and taking medication for this and that, conferring with so many doctors he could hardly keep them straight. One of them talked about a heart transplant.

He laughed. "At my age?" he said. "I'm 78. I don't think so."

When I talked to him on the phone in the fall of 2004 to tell him I would be on Oʻahu for a few weeks in October, he sounded good. But I still asked him how he was.

"Not good," he said.

"You sound good," I said.

"Well, I may sound OK, but I'm not good. I think I may never get back to Kalaupapa again. I am not good."

A couple of weeks later, I walked into his room at Hale Mohalu. When he saw me his face lit up in his beautiful, huge smile and he rolled himself back from a little table, pencil in hand.

I gave him a kiss and hug. "What are you working on?" I pointed to a paper napkin on the table he had covered with outline lettering: D I A L Y S I S.

"Oh, just a poster," he said. "Somebody wanted me to come speak at a dialysis meeting. I said I couldn't come but I would make art for them. I'm practicing the lettering. It will be 'Dialysis Is A Whale of A Deal.'" He held up the napkin, laid it down, and pulled a drawing from the pile of papers on the table.

On a five by seven board he'd drawn a humpback whale breaching off Kalaupapa's lighthouse point, the cliffs in the far background. For me the scene evoked the isolation and beauty of the peninsula, the raw power of the ocean and its creatures, and the feeling that what guides our lives is largely unseen.

Propped on the floor against the wall was a large framed oil painting of the whale, in an enlarged scene. A companion painting depicted the same whale underwater. The ethereal quality of it touched me even more.

I pointed to a stack of books, Westerns by Louis L'Amour and Zane Grey. "You're reading Zane Grey again," I said, remembering how he'd discovered the famous writer when he was a kid at Baldwin Home.

"I try to keep my mind occupied," he said. "But not with too heavy stuff. Over here at Hale Mohalu you go from your room to the kitchen, kitchen to room. The fourth time, you go crazy. I might have to commit myself." He laughed, but only a little.

Over a period of two weeks we worked on his last chapter, Chapter Seven. We conferred with a lawyer about the book. I reported to him my efforts to find a publisher. One day Monte—the photographer who had worked with us on the original magazine articles almost a decade ago—and I took Henry "riding," as he might say, to Waimea Falls on the North Shore. One evening Henry and I were among about 200 guests at a birthday party for a friend of his turning 50. Henry was asked to give the *pule*—the prayer —before dinner was served. He did, sonorous extemporaneous Hawaiian belying his declaration that his command of the spoken language came "two words at a time—and don't rush me."

In those weeks, I grew accustomed to walking across the Leahi Hospital lawn dodging morning sprinklers and enjoying the fragrance of plumeria trees in bloom. Hale Mohalu is at the *mākai* (ocean) end of the hospital campus, a little wing of an aging facility housing fewer and fewer aging patients. It's grown as geriatric as Kalaupapa itself.

But Hale Mohalu is closed in by a highrise hospital and the dry slopes of Diamond Head. The nearest beach, at Waikīkī, where Henry took his first saltwater swim the day before he left his mother forever, seems impossibly far away. Kalaupapa, prison though it was meant to be when the Kingdom established its quarantine leper settlement there in 1864, offers redemption as well as confinement in the sea and the cliffs, and a connection to the natural world—what Hawaiians call the *'āina*—that is so easy to sense in the sounds of the night and the winds of time.

Henry made it back to Kalaupapa for a time. Then his infamous left foot became such an infected problem that the only solution was to amputate the leg just below the knee. I visited him yet again at Hale Mohalu in late 2005.

One day when I was leaving, Henry showed me out to the sidewalk, paddling his wheelchair down the hallway and outside on the lānai, where the concrete is stained red with volcanic soil.

He stopped at the edge of the lawn and looked around. "Isn't this the saddest place?" he said.

What could I answer? I kissed him good-bye.

"*A hui hou*," he said. Until we meet again.

"*A hui hou*," I replied.

"Don't make it too long."

I thought of the last time he saw Cecile, how he made it quick, because he hates good-byes. *I think this is it.* I thought of how his dang-blasted ulcerated foot brought him the love of his life, his darling nurse, and how the same foot took her away. "*Henry, I don't love you anymore.*" I thought of him saying good-bye to his baby daughter only three days after she was born. *This was my baby, and she looked like a little angel.* I thought of him the day his mother left him at Kalihi Hospital. *I knew that she was crying and her heart was breaking.* I thought: He was feeling Annie Nalaielua's grief, leaving her youngest child at age ten when his only two sisters, Evelyn and Christina, had died only a few months before from the same dread disease.

I thought: It's no wonder Henry hates farewells.

So many years had passed since all those times, and here was my friend Henry at 79, the boy who thought he would do nothing more than drive the rubbish truck and die before he was 20.

I was tempted momentarily to wonder about "might have beens," but I came shortly to my senses. Gena recently repeated to me how much she values Henry's friendship, wisdom and mentoring. And then she added, "When he was a little boy of ten leaving his family for what would be his whole life, he thought he was going on an adventure. I think his 'adventure' will continue until the very end, since he's always looked at his life that way, no matter what."

Yes, Henry has spent all his life responding gloriously to the challenges dealt him. In that respect, he's like his hero Damien, the Blessed Damien.

Henry himself would not utter his own name and that of Damien in the same breath. And yet, in their later lives, each devoted himself to the same cause, each forged ahead in good spirit, no matter what.

"I don't think just anyone can understand all this about leprosy and Kalaupapa," Henry told me very near the end of our work on the book. "But you know, I think people today listen better." He paused. "I like talking about Kalaupapa. It's where my halo comes from."

And then he smiled at me, and, as he thought more about the halo, he laughed that beautiful baritone Hawaiian laugh. The echo of that rich, true laugh is my abiding experience of Henry, a laugh that somehow seems to come from beyond him, from a heart that is rooted in his spiritual home, the place where he found no footprints in the sand.

About the Authors

Henry Kalalahilimoku Nalaielua was raised in a sugar plantation community on the Big Island of Hawai'i until the age of ten. In 1936 he was diagnosed with what was then still called leprosy and was sent to Kalihi Hospital on the island of O'ahu and then to Kalaupapa, Moloka'i for indefinite confinement at a quarantine facility for Hansen's disease. Despite lifelong medical problems, Henry learned to draw and paint, to master 'ukulele and upright bass, and to turn his naturally inquisitive mind to learning. When the health facility at Kalaupapa was named a National Historical Park, he became a guide for park visitors. Henry has also served on numerous public agency advisory boards. He still lives at Kalaupapa.

Sally-Jo Keala-o-Ānuenue Bowman first worked with Henry in 1995, when he helped her with on-site research for several magazine articles about Kalaupapa. Her articles and essays have won several Pa'i Awards from the Hawaii Publishers Association and her prize-winning poetry and fiction have been published in a number of literary journals. She is a 1958 graduate of Kamehameha Schools and holds B.A. and M.S. degrees in journalism.

Index